ROUTLEDGE LIBRARY EDITIONS:
PEACE STUDIES

Volume 12

BUILDING THE INSTITUTIONS OF PEACE

BUILDING THE INSTITUTIONS OF PEACE
Swarthmore Lecture 1962

J. DUNCAN WOOD

Routledge
Taylor & Francis Group
LONDON AND NEW YORK

First published in 1962 by George Allen & Unwin Ltd

This edition first published in 2020
by Routledge
2 Park Square, Milton Park, Abingdon, Oxon OX14 4RN

and by Routledge
52 Vanderbilt Avenue, New York, NY 10017

Routledge is an imprint of the Taylor & Francis Group, an informa business

© 1962 Woodbrooke Council

All rights reserved. No part of this book may be reprinted or reproduced or utilised in any form or by any electronic, mechanical, or other means, now known or hereafter invented, including photocopying and recording, or in any information storage or retrieval system, without permission in writing from the publishers.

Trademark notice: Product or corporate names may be trademarks or registered trademarks, and are used only for identification and explanation without intent to infringe.

British Library Cataloguing in Publication Data
A catalogue record for this book is available from the British Library

ISBN: 978-0-367-21777-8 (Set)
ISBN: 978-0-429-29830-1 (Set) (ebk)
ISBN: 978-0-367-24377-7 (Volume 12) (hbk)
ISBN: 978-0-367-24388-3 (Volume 12) (pbk)
ISBN: 978-0-429-28219-5 (Volume 12) (ebk)

Publisher's Note
The publisher has gone to great lengths to ensure the quality of this reprint but points out that some imperfections in the original copies may be apparent.

Disclaimer
The publisher has made every effort to trace copyright holders and would welcome correspondence from those they have been unable to trace.

SWARTHMORE LECTURE 1962

THE SWARTHMORE LECTURES

1940. THE LIGHT OF CHRIST IN A PAGAN WORLD
    by John A. Hughes
1941. THE UNDIVIDED MIND
    by E. B. Castle
1942. THE LAW OF LIBERTY
    by Margaret M. Harvey
1943. PLANNING FOR FREEDOM
    by Leyton Richards
1944. MAN, SOCIETY AND RELIGION: AN ESSAY IN BRIDGE-BUILDING
    by W. Russell Brain
1945. WORSHIP AND SOCIAL PROGRESS
    by Wilfred Allott
1946. THE WARRANT FOR YOUTH'S SEARCH
    by John Hoare
1947. THE SALT AND THE LEAVEN
    by John W. Harvey
1949. AUTHORITY, LEADERSHIP AND CONCERN
    by Roger C. Wilson
1950. JUSTICE AND THE LAW OF LOVE
    by Konrad Braun
1951. QUAKERISM: A FAITH FOR ORDINARY MEN
    by R. Duncan Fairn
1952. PREPARATION FOR WORSHIP
    by Thomas F. Green
1953. REMOVING THE CAUSES OF WAR
    by Kathleen Lonsdale
1954. FROM LONELINESS TO FELLOWSHIP
    by Wilhelm Aarek
1955. WHERE WORDS COME FROM
    by Douglas V. Steere
1956. QUAKERS AND THE RELIGIOUS QUEST
    by Edgar G. Dunstan
1957. QUAKERISM AND EARLY CHRISTIANITY
    by Henry J. Cadbury
1958. THE CONCRETE AND THE UNIVERSAL
    by Margaret B. Hobling
1959. THE CASTLE AND THE FIELD
    by Harold Loukes
1960. THE CREATIVE IMAGINATION
    by Kenneth C. Barnes
1961. TOLERANCE AND THE INTOLERABLE
    by Richard K. Ullmann

SWARTHMORE LECTURE 1962

BUILDING
THE INSTITUTIONS
OF PEACE

BY

J. DUNCAN WOOD

LONDON
GEORGE ALLEN & UNWIN LTD
MUSEUM STREET

FIRST PUBLISHED IN 1962

This book is copyright under the Berne Convention. Apart from any fair dealing for the purpose of private study, research, criticism or review, as permitted under the Copyright Act, 1956, no portion may be reproduced by any process without written permission. Enquiries should be addressed to the Secretary, Swarthmore Lecture Committee, c/o Friends Home Service Committee, Friends House, Euston Road, London, N.W.1

© *Woodbrooke Council 1962*

PRINTED IN GREAT BRITAIN
in 11 on 12 point Baskerville type
BY HEADLEY BROTHERS LTD
109 KINGSWAY LONDON WC2
AND ASHFORD KENT

PREFACE

The Swarthmore Lectureship was established by the Woodbrooke Extension Committee at a meeting held December 7th, 1907; the minute of the Committee providing for "an annual lecture on some subject relating to the message and work of the Society of Friends". The name "Swarthmore" was chosen in memory of the home of Margaret Fox, which was always open to the earnest seeker after Truth, and from which loving words of sympathy and substantial material help were sent to fellow-workers.

The Lectureship has a twofold purpose; first, to interpret further to the members of the Society of Friends their Message and Mission; and, secondly, to bring before the public the spirit, the aims and the fundamental principles of the Friends. The Lecturer alone is responsible for any opinions expressed.

The Lectures have usually been delivered at the time of the assembly of London Yearly Meeting of the Society of Friends. The present Lecture, in abridged form, was delivered at Friends House, Euston Road, on the evening of May 25th, 1962.

A list of previous Lectures, as published in book form since 1940, will be found at the beginning of this volume, and those prior to 1940 at the end.

BIOGRAPHICAL NOTE

THOUGH not born a member of the Society of Friends, J. Duncan Wood was bred a Quaker and cherishes among his earliest memories a child's impression of Woodbrooke where his parents were Wardens. This was during the First World War, a time when even a small boy could appreciate the contrast between the patient promotion of peace within the Woodbrooke precincts and the furious pursuit of war without. He has since spent the greater part of his life within the precincts of Quaker institutions. Educated at Quaker schools, to which he owes among other debts his passion for bird-watching, he returned after graduating from Oxford University to teach at Leighton Park. His career as a schoolmaster was interrupted by wartime service with the Friends Ambulance Unit, three years of which were spent in China. Since 1952 he has been working at Geneva on the frontier where Quaker concerns meet those of an international world which, though employing different means, works for ends to which the Society of Friends is dedicated.

CONTENTS

I	*The Cave on Mount Horeb*	page	1
II	*From Penn to U.N.—Profit*		6
III	*From Penn to U.N.—Loss*		23
IV	*The Sands on which Peace has to be Built*		39
V	*East* v. *West* v. *the Rest*		47
VI	*The Dilemmas of International Co-operation*		66
VII	*The Small Voice of Prophecy*		84
Appendix I Extracts from William Penn's "Essay towards the Present and Future Peace of Europe" (Chapters VII and VIII)			97
Appendix II List of Abbreviations used in the Text			100

I
THE CAVE ON MOUNT HOREB

A QUAKER teacher of history remarked recently that he found it exhilarating to discuss world affairs with his senior pupils at a time when, as never before, we seem poised on the brink of eternity. Such joyful acceptance of being matched with the hour is as commendable as it is rare. Most of us tend to respond to humanity's present predicament with anxiety, frustration, indifference or apathy—anything but exhilaration. We feel that we have been matched with an hour more dreadful than any yet recorded and, though it is largely of our own creation, beg the Lord to take it away. But many generations have felt just the same, and we should not add to our anxieties by imagining ourselves to be unique. It is therefore helpful to remind ourselves of a very early crisis and consider what happened to the prophet Elijah when he found himself face to face with the powerful opposition of Jezebel and was forced to flee for his life to a cave on Horeb, the mount of God:

> And, behold, the Lord passed by, and a great and strong wind rent the mountains, and brake in pieces the rocks before the Lord; but the Lord was not in the wind: and after the wind an earthquake; but the Lord was not in the earthquake: and after the earthquake a fire; but the Lord was not in the fire: and after the fire a still small voice.
> And it was so, when Elijah heard it, that he wrapped his face in his mantle, and went out, and stood in the entering in of the cave. And, behold, there came a

> voice unto him, and said, What doest thou here, Elijah?
> And he said, I have been very jealous for the Lord God of hosts: because the children of Israel have forsaken thy covenant, thrown down thine altars, and slain thy prophets with the sword; and I, even I only, am left; and they seek my life, to take it away. And the Lord said unto him, Go, return on thy way to the wilderness of Damascus: and when thou comest, anoint Hazael to be king over Syria.
> And Jehu the son of Nimshi shalt thou anoint to be king over Israel: and Elisha the son of Shaphat of Abelmeholah shalt thou anoint to be prophet in thy room.[1]

Our familiarity with this incident is due in part to the reference made to it by John Greenleaf Whittier in lines which we sing as a hymn: "Speak through the earthquake, wind and fire, O still small voice of calm." We have, however, done Whittier an injustice by using as a hymn only the final stanzas of a longer poem[2] which is devoted to condemning the search for magical solutions to human problems. The stanzas that we sing are those in which he describes the Christian's openness to Divine influence and guidance in contrast to the pagan's total submission to a magic panacea. The poem opposes the "still small voice of calm" to the wild frenzy of intoxication; taken out of their context the lines we sing seem to us to be a call to quietism. If we look at the source of Whittier's lines, we find that the still small voice had a different message: the Lord did not suggest that Elijah should comfort himself in

[1] I Kings 19, 11-16.
[2] "The Brewing of Soma."

spiritual retirement; the still small voice was a call to action.

It is instructive to examine the action which Elijah was called upon to take: he was to make three appointments, two of them straight political appointments, the third to maintain the prophetic line. If, as I think it not altogether fanciful to suppose, we now find ourselves in a cave on Horeb, we, too, shall be sent on our way with a message compounded of politics and prophecy. Before we proceed to interpret our instructions, we must return again to the experience of Elijah. If we read a little further on in the Books of Kings we shall find that Elijah's political programme was not an unqualified success. Neither Hazael[1] nor Jehu[2] was a paragon of virtue or brought a lasting solution to the political problems which had baffled Elijah; certainly neither was a prince of peace. One is tempted to wonder whether Elijah misinterpreted the message which he heard: could it really be true that the Lord had selected two such violent and unruly princes to be His tools? The answer is that the Lord had no other choice. Amid the mediocre collection of men with whom He had to deal, these two fallible mortals were the best available. The Lord did not send a superman to remedy the situation, He chose Hazael and Jehu. So, today, the institutions which we now possess are the instruments at God's disposal and, halting, human and imperfect though they are, can be used for His purposes. If I understand aright Elijah's experience on Horeb, God would have us start from where we are.

He would also have us remember that the political

[1] II Kings 8, 15.
[2] II Kings 10, 31.

action which we undertake today will not automatically solve tomorrow's problem. For this reason the prophetic line has to be maintained against the day, which will come sooner rather than later, when Jehu and Hazael have fulfilled their mission and have lost touch with the problems of a new generation. It is the function of prophecy to interpret afresh the message of Horeb in the language that each generation understands, and in a manner relevant to the problems which it faces.

Another experience, for which I cannot give chapter and verse, may help us to see the dual nature of the Horeb message. It is recorded that a traveller in France once came upon a wayside hotel named "The Immaculate Conception and Commercial". This is a very apt name for the house in which the world lives and might appropriately be hung up as an inn-sign outside the Headquarters of United Nations. Human motives, whether expressed individually or collectively, are just such a mixture of the lofty and the base, the sacred and the profane, the sublime and the ridiculous. It is to this complexity that we have to address ourselves, and within the walls of this house that we have to live and work.

It is the function of a religious society to promote the lofty, the sacred and the sublime, which dwell on the upper floors of the house; it is also the duty of those who find their spiritual home upstairs to remain in constant touch with those who toil on the ground floor or in the basement. If the interests and concerns of the two levels of the house become so divergent that communication between them ceases altogether, we suffer a crisis of conscience of the kind our generation has experienced since the invention and use of nuclear weapons. At such times it is necessary to try to re-establish communication up and down the stairs. For this reason I take as the starting point for my remarks an early Quaker attempt to reconcile politics and prophecy, William Penn's "Essay Towards the Present and Future Peace of Europe".[1]

In this Essay, addressed to the princes of his day, Penn proposed a new political structure designed for the Europe which he knew but still astonishingly relevant to the world which we know. His proposals were, of course, revolutionary, but they were not utopian and they were not the pure milk of the Quaker word: they included a form of collective security and took very full account of the foibles and follies of his generation. At the same time the Essay is prophetic. It now has an honoured place in the long line of proposals, beginning with the "Grand Design" of Henry IV and Sully, to whom Penn acknowledged his debt, which has borne fruit in the present century. The Society of Friends has played some part in promoting the ideas expressed in Penn's Essay, though I suspect that even Friends have never given them all the attention they deserve. It is the purpose of this lecture to draw attention to them once more, to assess the progress that has been made in putting them into practice and to consider the next few steps that might be taken towards their more complete realization.

---

[1] Unfortunately now out of print.

II

FROM PENN TO U.N.—PROFIT

In putting forward his proposal for international co-operation, Penn was at pains to point out the "real benefits which would flow" from it. Subsequent history has justified his confidence: let us consider how the nations have been able, by agreement among themselves, to promote the "ease and security of travel" which Penn foresaw would flow from the adoption of his proposal. We are not, of course, concerned with the improvement in the material conditions of travel which has occurred since Penn visited the Continent with Fox and other English Friends in 1677, journeying by open wagon at immense discomfort and inconvenience. What does concern us is that the greater ease of modern methods of transportation has demanded an impressive degree of international co-operation unknown and unnecessary in Penn's time.[1] Whether he were to re-visit Europe by road, by rail, or by boat on the Rhine, his journey would be facilitated by numerous international agreements and conventions, designed to standardize equipment, to simplify formalities, or to open routes to international use. A list of conventions, published in 1948, mentions 53 relating to these three

---

[1] Travel was so slow in Penn's day that Europe had not yet found it necessary to agree upon a uniform calendar. Most Catholic states had adopted the New Style of Pope Gregory XIII, but many Protestant states, including Great Britain, adhered to the Old Style. In Germany the calendar was a patchwork following the religion of the ruler of each state.

modes of travel, the earliest dating from 1856; but the list neither reveals nor estimates the diplomatic labour usefully devoted to arriving at these agreements for the general benefit of mankind.

If Penn were to re-visit Pennsylvania by sea, he would profit from an even larger body of international legislation, which was already in slow process of formation in his own day. The doctrine of the freedom of the seas, first formulated by Grotius in 1609, means that, if the sea belongs equally to all, the rights and duties of all thereon must be defined by common agreement. Between 1857 and 1948 sixty international conventions were drawn up concerning maritime navigation, covering a wide range of subjects from maritime signals and collisions at sea to sanitary and safety regulations, many of which are the continuing concern of the youngest of the Specialized Agencies.[1] United Nations has recently assisted in the codification of maritime law, and if two plenipotentiary conferences failed to agree on the difficult problem of the width of territorial waters, this should not blind us to their solid achievements in other, less controversial areas. Since the oceans cover more than two-thirds of the globe, it can be claimed that a much larger portion of the earth's surface is governed by agreed international law than remains outside its jurisdiction.

The long experience in legislating for the ocean has been applied to air travel, whose international implications were obvious from its inception. These are regu-

---

[1] The International Maritime Consultative Organization (IMCO) which started work in 1959. One of the latest conventions with which IMCO is concerned seeks to prevent the pollution of the sea by oil. This will benefit fish and birds as well as mankind.

lated by another Specialized Agency,[1] which is responsible for the drafting of international air traffic conventions and provides a forum for the discussion of measures to promote the safety of civil aviation. The degree of safety which this mode of travel now enjoys would not be possible without the close co-operation and constant research of the World Meteorological Organization, a Specialized Agency whose area of competence is one where national barriers are meaningless and where no progress can be made without international co-operation.

There is another, related, area in which Penn would note progress, that of communications. International conventions relating to postal services, and to telegraph, telephone and radio, have been negotiated largely under the auspices of the two relevant Specialized Agencies, the Universal Postal Union and the International Telecommunications Union. It may be claimed that these two unspectacular bodies have as great an influence over our daily life as any other UN organ, being ultimately responsible for the arrangements which bring us our foreign mail and fill our newspapers with despatches from foreign correspondents. They have done much to promote another of those "real benefits" which Penn envisaged, in that they help to "beget and increase personal friendship".

With very few exceptions, the spheres of international co-operation mentioned above did not exist in Penn's time and he could not have foreseen their development. Most of them result from the scientific and technological advances of the past hundred years or more, and it can be claimed with some justification that it was

[1] The International Civil Aviation Organization (ICAO), established in 1947.

in the very nature of science and technology to create their own international structures. At an early stage in the development of modern methods of transport and communications further progress became impossible without international co-operation: thus, ITU dates from 1865 and UPU from 1875; though WMO was not established until 1951, it succeeded the International Meteorological Organization, set up in 1878 and itself the result of co-operation between meteorologists which had started 25 years earlier. Indeed, this form of co-operation is but the continuation of the brotherhood of science which had defied national frontiers, and even wars, during the 18th century, and was a particular manifestation of the concept of the unity of Europe. Napoleon gave considerable impetus to this concept by bringing to those parts of the Continent which he conquered common institutions, among them the decimal system of weights and measures, so that both tradition and practical considerations favoured the development of co-operation between European nations.

Yet Napoleon had also aroused contrary tendencies by stimulating nationalism which emphasized the divisions of Europe. In spite of this background of separatism the international institutions to which reference has been made were created to meet the over-riding needs of the time. It has further to be remembered that many of the international conventions which laid the foundations of international co-operation in these spheres involved real or supposed economic sacrifices for those who ratified them. The standardization of equipment, for instance, may involve the dismantling of national installations which represent a certain capital investment.[1] It requires a long-term view of one's economic advantage, or of one's international responsibility, to be prepared to make such sacrifices.

Great as are the benefits which we derive from improvements internationally promoted in travel and communications, to lay stress upon these may be to miss Penn's point: what really concerned him was the hindrance to travel and traffic presented by the numerous "stops and examinations" at frontiers. He assumed that, if the princes of Europe created among themselves a "diet, parliament or estates", much of the nuisance of frontiers would disappear, and that Europeans would then recover the freedom of movement which they enjoyed in Roman times, without the burden of supporting the central Roman bureaucracy. In this Penn seems to have been over-optimistic. He intended the princes of Europe to retain their internal sovereignty after they became members of the European Diet, but forgot that of all the manifestations of sovereignty, the most persistent is the desire to check travellers and levy customs duties at the frontier. Other close alliances comparable to that which Penn proposed for Europe have not automatically led to the abandonment of this sovereign right. Thus the 38 sovereign states which formed the German Confederation in 1815 retained their independent tariffs and the control of their

[1] For example, WMO recently decided that for international purposes temperatures should be recorded in Celsius or centigrade. The United Kingdom much preferred Fahrenheit, both from national habit and because it held that Fahrenheit is a more sensible system. It has, however, accepted the majority decision in favour of Celsius, and as from January 1st, 1961, changed all its thermometers accordingly, only retaining the use of Fahrenheit in weather forecasts to the British public.

frontiers until economic pressures from their most powerful member forced them to join a customs union; the Swiss cantons, which began their education in the art of co-operation as long ago as 1291, retained their individual rights to levy customs duties until the reform of the Confederation of 1848.

In fact, in the sense of freedom from frontier control, the "ease and security of travel and traffic" has steadily diminished from Penn's time until our own. If the number of European frontiers has been greatly reduced by the unification of Germany and Italy, their significance has, over most of this period, enormously increased as a result of the greater power invested in the State and the much greater efficiency with which this power is wielded. This has not merely restricted the ease of travel and traffic, it has in many instances given the State power over life and death by enabling it to refuse asylum to political refugees, an inhuman exercise of sovereign rights which has reached its peak in the present century. Only in the last few years has a sudden and dramatic retreat from this position been witnessed in Western Europe, but not yet, alas, in Eastern Europe. The abolition of visas, and in some cases of passports, has been followed by a progressive lowering of tariff walls and by the first steps towards a Common Market whose creation would have appeared to most people only 30 years ago to be not merely impossible, but actually undesirable.

It will be objected that the creation of the Common Market is no more than a natural consequence of a development which requires larger economic units, just as, at an earlier stage in the industrial revolution, the German Zollverein and the abolition of cantonal tolls in Switzerland were natural and inevitable. But these changes do not simply happen of themselves. Some human volition is required. The Common Market was originally the concept of a few highly placed ministers. The experts who were asked to draft the Treaty of Rome at first reported that the operation was impossible, and only changed their minds when informed from above that, impossible or no, it had to be done. But human volition at the top is not enough: the ultimate success of such an experiment depends on its ability to mitigate the sacrifices demanded from its weaker members and to create a favourable climate of public opinion towards all its consequences, whether they be beneficial or painful. One of the consequences of the Common Market may well be a return to the "fluidity" of the labour market which still existed 100 years or more ago, but has gradually been checked by the rise of exclusive national states. It remains to be seen whether the members of the Common Market will readily accept workers from their less prosperous neighbours or whether, as a result of the nationalist indoctrination of the past few generations, they will treat them with a scorn which Penn would have found both repugnant and incomprehensible. We cannot expect to enjoy the economic advantages of new conditions without changing our patterns of thought—and even relinquishing cherished traditions—in order to keep pace with them—a lesson which, it seems, has still to be learned in Great Britain.

Remarkable though this revolution in European sentiment is, it has the disadvantage of being limited in scope to only a part of one continent, and of being designed, to some extent, as a defensive measure against pressure from outside—just as Penn thought of his own plan as a defence against possible renewal of invasion by the Turks. It is too soon to say whether its defensive aspect will make the new Europe self-seeking and exclusive or whether its co-operative aspect will enable it to contribute to world peace. Neither result is inevitably bound up with the existing constitution; all will depend on the leadership that is forthcoming from the nations which make it up.

However, neither the European Common Market, nor other regional economic unions now under consideration, tell the whole story of the new trend in promoting ease and security of traffic. Though we have failed so far to establish the International Trade Organization, we do possess a body of limited membership but world-wide scope for the discussion of commercial questions, the General Agreement on Tariffs and Trade. Surprising though this institution would be to Penn, in whose days the control of trade was regarded as one of the most important weapons in the armoury of sovereign states, he would recognize in it many of the features which he proposed for the maintenance of peace in the political field. It is in essence a parliament of states, committed to the promotion of international trade by the reduction of customs barriers and the maintenance of fair practices, a parliament in which each of the contracting parties can state his problems, request or offer concessions, and adjust his differences with his fellow members by a process of patient and prolonged negotiation. It further resembles Penn's Diet in having a very small secretariat whose duty is to facilitate the work which is performed by the member governments themselves.

The GATT has the disadvantage that it is far from universal and cannot easily include among its contracting parties states which do not conduct their foreign commerce in accordance with the established practices of a free enterprise system; but it has the immense advantage of putting an end to the tariff wars which, as recently as 1939, were among the important contributory causes of armed hostilities. This agreement has worked well in conditions of expanding trade; it remains to be seen how well its principles will be maintained against the pressures of a prolonged recession.

I have dwelt at length on the benefits to travel and traffic which Penn expected to flow from his proposal, because these are the fruits of international co-operation which we all enjoy, even in a prosperous country like Britain where it can be too easily assumed that United Nations and its Agencies are irrelevant and costly luxuries. The numerous other benefits which Penn foretold and which the world is now beginning to enjoy must be dealt with more briefly. They are to be found in almost every sphere, economic, humanitarian, social and political, and in very many cases are promoted by institutions specially created for the purpose.

Several examples of international co-operation in economic questions have already been given, but there remains a vast and important field of international endeavour, the promotion of the economic development of newly independent countries. For this purpose we have created the Bank,[1] the Food and Agriculture

[1] The International Bank for Reconstruction and Development, established in 1945.

Organization and others, and have elaborated programmes of Technical Assistance through which the skills which modern science has developed, mostly in the industrialized countries, can be of service to poorer nations struggling against ignorance, hunger and disease. Contributions to these programmes do not come exclusively from the rich: few nations are, in fact, so poor that they cannot contribute to this programme some skill or competence in return for what they receive, so that it is an inspiring exercise in human co-operation and one of the outstanding achievements of the twentieth century.

In the field of humanitarian endeavour our international effort began with the establishment nearly 100 years ago of the International Red Cross, an instrument for maintaining the principles of humanity in the midst of the inhumanity of warfare and a channel for the expression of international charity moved by the sufferings of victims of disasters. We have also slowly established inter-governmental machinery to deal with the needs of refugees, a problem with which Penn was familiar as he witnessed the flight of the Huguenots from France. As a result of the strengthening of frontiers and of the nationalism which stands behind them, refugees in our own day have had a colder welcome than was accorded to the Huguenots, and we have been slow to recognize that national exclusiveness must be compensated by the recognition of international responsibility. This responsibility may be discharged hesitatingly but the Arab refugees, for example, miserable though their lot is, may be considered fortunate to have been within the reach of aid from an international community prepared to respond to their needs.[1] But governments, even within the international bodies which they have created, regard the refugee as primarily a political phenomenon and it is left to Voluntary Agencies to treat him as a homeless brother.

It is in the matter of the improvement of social conditions that we have the greatest proliferation of international institutions, ranging from Specialized Agencies, such as the International Labour Organization, the World Health Organization and UNESCO, to UN congresses summoned to discuss a specific topic or to draw up an international convention relating to it. Two subjects in which the Society of Friends has taken a close interest, the abolition of slavery and the slave trade, and penal reform, may be taken as examples of international co-operation in social matters. The slave trade, being a form of international commerce, can only be effectively controlled by the active co-operation of governments. Britain led in this matter by abolishing the slave trade unilaterally in 1807, but it was over 80 years before the influence of her example was translated into the Brussels Convention of 1890.[2] Unfortunately, in spite of this Convention the institution of slavery still persists in certain parts of the world and where there is a slave market traders will find ways and means of supplying it. In former times the existence of slavery in a particular territory was made

---

[1] More fortunate than the Armenians in the First World War or the Germans at the end of the Second, to whose fate the international community remained indifferent, and, of course, far more fortunate than the Jews of Hitler's Europe, who were beyond the reach of international intervention.

[2] Britain's unilateral lead was, perhaps, compromised by the fact that the enforcement of the international convention which she proposed in 1815 would have fallen to the British navy, a prospect which other powers viewed with alarm.

the excuse for its occupation by a colonial power;[1] today the means of dealing with what is regarded as a matter of domestic jurisdiction are more limited: world public opinion may be roused and may, eventually, result in a slave-owning country asking for assistance in the abolition of the institution,[2] a slower process than conquest, but in the long run much more sure.

With the exception of international criminals, for whose control special agreements exist, penal reform is a matter solely of domestic jurisdiction and therefore beyond the scope of international conventions. Friends were among the first to spread internationally new ideas about the treatment of offenders and the early Quaker pioneers would rejoice to know that questions so dear to their hearts are now discussed at United Nations congresses by representatives of numerous governments anxious to benefit from one another's experience. Such discussions are fruitful in so far as those present, whatever their political allegiance, recognize that the problems of human psychology cannot be met by ready-made doctrinaire solutions and that crime is a burden common to all societies whatever their guiding ideology. There are many other social questions—for example, the emancipation of women—in which reform can best be promoted in international discussion from which each participating country may derive ideas suited to its own conditions. It is not always necessary, or even desirable, that such discussion should result in a binding international convention;

[1] This is the origin of the Belgian presence in the Congo and, as recently as 1935, was used by Mussolini as an excuse for his invasion of Ethiopia.
[2] Liberia took action of this kind in 1929.

the most that can be agreed upon may be a general declaration or recommendation, indicating desirable standards of legislation but recognizing that the day of their universal application is still remote.[1]

Nevertheless, international conventions have been an important vehicle of progress in every sphere of activity, technological, economic, humanitarian, social and political. Every such international agreement voluntarily entered into by a state constitutes a limitation on that state's sovereign freedom of action. Consequently, the ratification of any convention, in whatever field, is a political act and its continued observance will be determined by political considerations. The most potent political consideration favouring the observance of conventions is the pressure of a public opinion ready to remind governments of the obligations which they have voluntarily undertaken and to insist that a nation's true interest coincides with its international responsibility. There is no other ultimate sanction—other than war—for the sanctity of treaties, for the International Court of Justice which crowns an imposing edifice of international law can utter opinions and make judgments but has, as yet, no power to enforce their acceptance.

[1] The ILO, which has elaborated numerous conventions to regulate hours and conditions of labour, is laying increasing stress on recommendations which do not have the same binding force. The best known example of a general recommendation is the Universal Declaration of Human Rights adopted by United Nations in 1948. The attempt to transform this declaration of "desirable standards" into binding conventions has so far failed owing to the wide divergencies in the political philosophies of UN members. The 16 members of the Council of Europe who share common political traditions have, however, been able to put into operation a European Convention of Human Rights which permits citizens to appeal to a European Court against their governments; several have already done so.

Eventually, Penn's tour of modern international organizations would take him to New York to examine the embodiment of his own proposals. He would not take long to discover that United Nations has adopted some of his suggestions almost in their original form. There are, for instance, précis-writers, there are summary records of the debates made available to all the delegates, there are official languages—admittedly five, not one or two as he proposed—and there is a two-thirds majority rule which seems to be a compromise between Penn's alternative proposals. His suggestion for rotating chairmanship is not carried out entirely on the lines which he proposed, but the principle is accepted. On the other hand, his refusal to accept abstentions in the vote has not been maintained; nor has it been felt necessary, except in the election of the President, to insist on vote by secret ballot. We may pride ourselves that we no longer need this protection against corruption, though we have to admit that the present system of voting does encourage the use of certain other forms of pressure and persuasion. We might also pride ourselves on the fact that the numerous doors into the Assembly are there for convenience, not "to avoid quarrel for precedency", a very important question in Penn's day for which he quite justifiably made provision.[1] Here again, we should have to explain that the vexed question of precedency has for the present at least been solved by such devices

[1] In the 17th century the exaggerated importance attached to "the most absurd and quibbling points of etiquette and precedence" frequently delayed diplomatic negotiations—notably, and tragically, those which terminated the Thirty Years War which had to be conducted in two separate cities in order to satisfy the self-esteem of the French and the Swedes.

as permanent seats on the Security Council, "equitable geographical distribution", and "a reasonable share in the official functions". The problem is not dead, but it has been transformed; an achievement on which Penn might be inclined to congratulate us. It is doubtful whether he would be equally impressed with the standard of behaviour in debate, where he felt no precaution to be necessary—"the liberty and rule of speech, to be sure, they cannot fail in". In this respect, we seem to live in decadent times.

Penn would be surprised to learn that this Diet is not an alliance of princes, nor established, like its predecessor, by "high contracting parties", but founded upon a Charter, which begins with the words "We, the peoples". Cynics would inform him that these words are a device to give a semblance of democracy to a heterogeneous collection of governments, many of them far from representative of their subjects; they would commend the formula used by the League of Nations as more realistic. Such an extreme view has to be modified by recognition of certain other facts, such as the contribution made by private, non-governmental organizations to the drawing up of the Charter at San Francisco. This contact between the private citizen and the governmental delegate has been preserved and provided for in the Charter and has on occasion influenced United Nations policy. For example, the establishment of the Economic Commission for Africa may be attributed in part to the pressure of certain Non-Governmental Organizations; World Refugee Year is another instance of the influence of private initiative on international action, and recently other methods[1] have been evolved for the direct participation of individuals in the work of United Nations. This is a development which owes more to the principles which Penn propounded in the Frame of Government for Pennsylvania than to the proposals which he made in his Essay.

We have passed in review a portion of the remarkable group of international institutions with which the world is now endowed, covering between them almost every aspect of human life, activity and aspiration. What judgment would Penn pronounce on the achievement which this represents? He would first observe that the bulk of the institutions which have been described are not restricted to Europe, but are worldwide; of this he would surely approve. Next he would note that the earliest effective international institutions grew up to promote co-operation in technological and scientific fields and that, on the whole, such institutions have benefited from having a limited and clearly defined objective.[2] He would judge that science and technology have been most amenable to international direction, social questions somewhat less, economic questions less still, and political questions least of all. He would record the contribution made to the establishment of these institutions by visionaries such as

[1] For example, the initiative of the Friends of Urbana-Champaign Meeting (Illinois) in imposing on themselves a voluntary tax of 1 per cent. of their income has been widely followed by Friends and others in the United States, Canada and Mexico. In this way Friends alone have contributed more than £20,000 to the UN Technical Assistance Programme for its work in Africa.

[2] Thus, the experience of WHO, which has a clearly defined field of action, has been happier than that of UNESCO whose activities are dispersed over many fields.

Dunant, founder of the Red Cross, by leaders such as Albert Thomas of the ILO, and Dag Hammarskjöld of United Nations, and by countless others, less well-known, who devoted their lives to the conception or the creation of this machinery for peace. He would note that the machinery was not created at a single moment of history, but was built up gradually piece by piece, as necessity demanded. He would be told that the greatest impetus to this growth has been given by two disastrous world wars, from both of which peoples and governments emerged determined to root out the causes of war; and that the institutions created for this purpose showed on the second occasion a deeper understanding of the problem than on the first. He would thus recognize that the accumulated experience of mankind has fully corroborated the wisdom of his proposals; and he would be happy to find that the arguments in favour of peace which he painstakingly expounded in his Essay are accepted as axioms, that everyone now acknowledges the "real benefits" which peace can bestow, so that an important part of his Essay is no longer necessary. Penn would next ask why, if this is now the case, so little real progress has been made in making these benefits lasting and secure.

III
FROM PENN TO U.N.—LOSS

IMPRESSIVE though the existing international structure is, it should not blind us to the fact that it in no wise accomplishes Penn's objective: the outlawry of war. That the structure is useful there can be no doubt, for some of it has survived two world wars and much of it one, to be recreated, improved and extended immediately after the end of hostilities. But the mere fact that these interruptions occurred shows that international agreement on social, economic, humanitarian or technological problems, will not of itself prevent war; this would only be true if such problems were the primary concern of states, which at present is far from being the case. Furthermore, to dwell too long or to dwell exclusively on the many achievements of United Nations and its Agencies in the social, economic and humanitarian fields obscures the fact that the real importance of United Nations lies in the political field. If UN cannot achieve anything here, it will sooner or later collapse, and we shall be left with a number of Agencies, of undoubted but limited utility, promoting well-being but powerless to produce peace. Unfortunately, such a development is precisely what many people desire.[1]

[1] For example, the writer of a letter to the *Daily Telegraph* for January 16th, 1962, suggests that "we should bow ourselves out from UN's political organizations, preserving, if practically possible, the UN Agencies such as WHO, FAO, ECOSOC (*sic*), etc.". This ignores the fact that UN was created on the correct assumption that peace must have economic as well as political bases which are closely intertwined. For this reason ECOSOC was created as a Principal Organ (*not* an "Agency") of UN and its debates are profoundly influenced by political considerations.

Although the popular support which UN now enjoys is considerable it would be extremely dangerous to exaggerate its effectiveness. All too frequently public opinion regards United Nations and its Agencies as remote ivory towers, inhabited by theorists who indulge in a great deal of talk at the taxpayer's expense but perform very little work of practical value. This is extremely remote from the truth, but the misconception is likely to persist since it is but the extension to the international plane of the notions often harboured about the seat of national government.[1] A more serious popular misconception is to refer continually to United Nations as "it", implying that the institution is something remote from and independent of its component parts. It is true that any international body creates a character and a dynamism of its own, which gives it a life apart from the nations which belong to it, so that the whole is greater than the sum of the parts which compose it. Nevertheless, it is incorrect to ask, as people often do, "what is UN doing about it?"; the question should be phrased: "What are *we* doing about it, through our agency, UN?" The detachment, which is widely felt, between "We, the peoples" and the institution which they are credited with creating, makes it possible for the leader of a great nation, which has contributed much in the past to international thought, to refer contemptuously to United Nations as a "machin",[2] and to incur relatively little criticism for so doing. In fact, whenever a decision is taken in one

[1] Thus the Swiss, whose country is a United Nations in miniature, refer with more or less tolerant amusement to the "chaps in Berne", and frequently reject the legislation which these "chaps" propose for their benefit.
[2] "Contraption."

or other of the organs of UN which appears to run counter to the interests of an individual nation, especially of one which has pretensions to greatness, it is easy enough to excite popular feeling against it. The Suez crisis of 1956 at first roused a good deal of support for UN amongst certain sections of the British public, but the net result seems to have been a decline in support, when it became clear that it would not be possible for United Nations to achieve those British aims which had precipitated the crisis in the first place.

It must be remembered that these national reactions have occurred in countries well-informed about the purposes of United Nations and predisposed by training and experience to the acceptance of such an institution. A great many member nations do not have this background to their international thinking; consequently, their notions of the responsibilities of UN membership are still at a primitive level. In two big crises, Suez in 1956, Congo in 1960, the machinery of United Nations has been used to stem or to limit a conflict. In each case the solution, approved by large majorities, has involved additional financial contributions, but a large number of states have shirked the obligations which their support for the action in question has implied.[1] The numerous states who have defaulted on their assessment for the Congo operation justify themselves on the ground that they agreed to pay for an action which they had conceived on quite different lines, but no such excuse can be put forward for the defaulters in payments for UNEF, prominent among whom are to be found the Soviet Union and

[1] It is estimated that by September, 1962, the total deficit on these operations will be of the order of £70,000,000.

its allies, who claim that the costs of an action from which they greatly benefited should be borne solely by those who provoked it. Though in these instances this attitude must presumably seem justifiable to those who adopt it, no excuse can be made for the states who are in arrears on their ordinary contributions to the regular UN budget, who, at the end of 1959, numbered twelve out of eighty.

It is doubtless irksome for a state to be obliged to contribute to a special UN fund in order to repair mistakes made by fellow-members, but this does not apply to voluntary contributions made to extra-budgetary funds. Political considerations have restricted the number of contributors to UN's programmes for refugees,[1] but UNICEF, the Expanded Programme of Technical Assistance and the UN Special Fund have enjoyed a much wider range of support, as a result of the example set by some member states and of the fact that these programmes have proved their worth. Indeed, the high degree of international solidarity achieved in support of this work is commendable. One is therefore reluctant to look a gift horse in the mouth, but if one does, one finds that the total of economic aid channelled through UN organs in this

---

[1] The socialist states have always voted against any appropriation for the office of the UN High Commissioner for Refugees, whose principal pre-occupation has been for refugees from eastern Europe. They approve, however, of the High Commissioner's programme on behalf of the refugees from Algeria to which France, to her credit, is a major contributor. The Arab refugees, to whose support Israel has made some contributions, make a more unequivocal call upon the conscience of the international community: yet their livelihood has been assured almost entirely by the United States (70 per cent.) and the British Commonwealth (20 per cent.). The Soviet Union has not contributed a penny to this operation which has played an important part in maintaining peace in the Middle East.

way by the great powers represents only a fraction of what they have devoted to their own bilateral programmes. They justify this policy to themselves on the ground that bilateral aid can be given without international scrutiny, that one can be certain it is directed towards one's old friends, or towards making new ones, and that it provides a better safeguard for national interests than does the multilateral UN system.

Unfortunately, the policy adopted for economic aid is also followed in political questions. To date, three attempts have been made to put into operation a system of collective security such as Penn proposed in his Essay. The great powers who formed first the Holy Alliance, then the League of Nations, and finally United Nations, two of whom figure in all three experiments, have felt that their security could not be assured by a collective system alone, and have had recourse to alliances of a more selective kind. This means that collective security has scarcely ever been put to the test, since a system of alliances destroys the unanimity of opposition to any state which is judged a transgressor. When the system produces two equally powerful and close-knit alliances, as at the present time, Penn's conclusion no longer holds that "all the other sovereignties, united as one strength, shall compel the submission and performance of the sentence . . . no sovereignty in Europe having the power and therefore cannot show the will to dispute the conclusion".

It is unlikely that the League of Nations could have overcome this handicap, even if it had been a more universal body than was actually the case. If United Nations has succeeded in co-existing with the alliances which make its own life so precarious, it is due in large measure to the reluctance of the opposing power groups to go to war. It has thus been the task of United Nations to insulate disputes and prevent them from involving the major powers in a direct conflict. This has been an invaluable service, and, incidentally, a very much cheaper form of security than the alliances, but it has not led to a satisfactory solution of all the problems in question as is witnessed by the long list of unresolved issues with which the Security Council is currently seized.[1] In the long run United Nations cannot survive on a basis of merely holding matters in suspense.

The Congo crisis illustrates very well both the potentialities and the grave shortcomings of United Nations. In the economic, social and technical aspects of its work United Nations has achieved some success—considering the circumstances, a remarkable degree of success; but in its political aspects the action has failed to produce the results expected of it. Thus in its Congo operation UN faithfully mirrors mankind's maturity and immaturity in the art of co-operation. Even from the point of view of a purely technical assistance operation, Congo presented some unprecedented difficulties. In July 1960 the whole machinery of government of a country as large as Western Europe fell to pieces. This has never happened before with such dramatic suddenness; but when governments have collapsed in the past the problem has been "solved" by war, either civil or international. It is extremely

[1] The "summary statement on matters of which the Security Council is seized" issued on December 5th, 1961, lists 52 items, many of them, admittedly, no longer live issues. Some of them are pathetic last-minute protests against what have long since been accepted as *faits accomplis*.

fortunate for Congo that there existed a body able, even if not adequately equipped, to come to the rescue. What the situation really demanded was the application on a large scale of the scheme known as "OPEX", under which senior government officials are lent by the more highly-developed countries to work in the ministries of less developed countries where the practice and principles of administration are not well understood. This is a scheme in which Dag Hammarskjöld took a very close personal interest and for which he had obtained the sanction of a somewhat hesitant Economic and Social Council. Unfortunately, the scheme was still in its infancy when the Congo crisis broke, demanding the recruitment of a far larger number of advisers than were provided for under the whole of the OPEX programme. In any case the recruitment of OPEX officers takes time, and in order to meet the emergency it was necessary to despatch to the Congo members of the Secretariat responsible for administering other programmes of UN and the Specialized Agencies—many of whom volunteered their services—thus putting a heavy strain on the whole of the international civil service. Inevitably there were members of ONUC who did not measure up to the unfamiliar tasks to which they were called, and it has come as a shock to many, notably and illogically those who constantly criticize the costliness of United Nations, that the organization could not discover in its various offices a larger number of brilliant extempore administrators. Such men are unfortunately not so plentiful that numbers of them can be kept idle waiting for an emergency; those in UN can ill be spared and few national administrations are overburdened with them. The critics of UN's work in civil administration also pay too little attention to the extraordinary limitations which the Congo situation put upon it. Technical assistance is given only at the request of a government and in accordance with its wishes; in Congo the government was too young to have formulated precise wishes and was frequently not there to express them in any case. Furthermore, the Congolese had become so aroused against their white masters that they treated all white men with suspicion or contempt, including the representatives of UN.

All these difficulties might have been overcome had there been clarity about UN's political mission. For the short period at the beginning of the crisis when there was a measure of agreement on policy there was a strong sense of purpose about the whole operation. The emergence of sharp disagreement in the Security Council resulted in destroying this sense of purpose and in forcing United Nations personnel to carry out only the minimum action on which agreement could be found. It is probably not fully appreciated how big a strain this put on the men who served in Congo and how loyally they fulfilled their instructions not to use force, even when the situation seemed to offer no other solution. None of the numerous nations who supported the UN operation would have undertaken a national policy on such terms. A national expedition "to restore law and order" would not only have used force, it would have been supported by a coherent body of (possibly mistaken) opinion at home. The supporting opinion for the UN forces was personified by Mr. Hammarskjöld who eventually lost his life in the service of principles which he properly regarded as being above national interests; but these principles had not aroused sufficiently widespread support to provide the solid encouragement which is required by a group of men facing an unfamiliar situation in very difficult circumstances.

The weakness of the support for the principles of international action was revealed as one nation after another began to adopt an independent Congo policy of its own, pursuing its national interests while, in some cases, continuing publicly to support UN action. It may be that the Congolese people would be happier now if they had been forced to accept any one of a number of solutions to their problems gratuitously offered by great, medium and small powers alike, and promoted within Congo by methods incompatible with the principle of non-intervention imposed on United Nations itself. All of these nations, and they include several of the great powers, have criticized the inadequacy or even the existence, of the international machinery for dealing with the situation. The criticism should really be directed at the inadequacy of their own sense of international responsibility.

It is dangerous to write of a crisis so recent as that of Congo and one which, at the time of writing, is still very far from solution. The risk has been taken because developments in Congo have already provided an illustration of the principal problems which at present jeopardize the prospects of establishing an effective international organization. These may be described as the "North-South" and the "East-West" problems.

The "North-South" question is a complex of problems, political, economic and psychological, which disturb the relationships between the prosperous industrialized countries of the temperate zone and the under-developed countries of the tropical and subtropical regions. One of the encouraging aspects of this question is the relative painlessness—as compared with the history of nation-building in Europe—of the process of emancipation which has given birth to 42 new sovereign states since the end of the Second World War. The discouraging aspect is that the offspring of this process are so ill provided with the attributes of sovereignty, political strength and economic viability. This weakness creates a deep gulf between the weak and the strong, the poor and the rich, which can be bridged only by a sustained effort on the part of the new states and by aid from without. Such aid may come from the former colonial powers, but it is psychologically difficult for the new states to ask for it from that quarter, the more so as it risks limiting the new political independence by economic dependence; it is also psychologically difficult for the former colonial powers to grant this aid, especially when they are expected to do so in expiation of sins which their fathers committed under the impression that they were virtues. The alternative, namely seeking aid from the United States or the Soviet Union, involves considerable political risks for the new states and great political temptations for the two great powers. In these circumstances the newly independent countries are bound to look to United Nations as the best source of the economic aid which they so urgently need and of the protection against aggression which they are manifestly unable to provide from their own resources.

The fact that United Nations is not properly equipped to provide the aid and protection which the newly-independent countries require is due to the influence of the other besetting problem of our time, the ideological conflict between East and West. The quasi-religious fervour with which this struggle is conducted invites comparison with that between Catholic and Protestant in the sixteenth and seventeenth centuries, but the two conflicts are fundamentally different. Of course, post-Reformation Europe was divided into two camps as post-revolution Europe is today, but the camps were not two sharply opposed political blocks. Even at the height of the religious struggle dynastic interests had become quite as important as religious ones, and by Penn's time the religious differences had so far lost their importance as a source of international tension that he does not refer to them in his Essay. He was legislating for a group of princes and governments who, whether Catholic or Protestant, shared common traditions and outlook. So far had the crusading spirit died away that it did not even occur to him that the inclusion of the Orthodox Russians and the Moslem Turks, which he proposed, would have introduced incompatible elements.

There is a somewhat closer parallel between the present ideological struggle and the conflicts arising from the ideological nationalism of the nineteenth and twentieth centuries. The development of the modern state would not have been possible without the creation of ideologies more powerful than simple loyalty to a prince, which could provide a purpose and a mission to justify the increased ardour and tempo of the national life. What had previously been historic communities were transformed by this process into self-conscious nations. The two ideologies now in conflict began by being the agents of just such a transformation, creating nations out of disparate and heterogeneous elements; in China the Communist Party is performing the same task of transformation which was left unfinished by its predecessors. But other modern states have been created on the basis of a purely national ideology, stressing the exclusive aspects of the nation and erecting around it barriers all the more impenetrable for being founded largely upon myth. Nationalism may have been a satisfactory foundation for a state in the nineteenth century, but its survival into the twentieth produced the holocaust of National Socialism, a doctrine incompatible with any form of international organization or recognized political morality.

Nationalism was by nature exclusive, and Fascism and Nazism were both, at one time, labelled "not for export"; the ideologies with which we now have to deal, though nationally based, are intended to be universal in their application. They stem from a body of thought to which Christians, non-Christians and anti-Christians have all made contributions and they have given birth to political institutions comparable to the First French Republic whose slogan "Liberté, Egalité, Fraternité" conveyed a universal message and, incidentally, enabled it to extend its frontiers and its power. Such a combination of national interest with a world-wide mission is an essential and complicating factor in the current ideological struggle. There was much substance in the French claim to have a message for mankind, but it has led them to assume that the Frenchman is a "universal man" whose civilization and culture are the goal and aspiration of the human race, an assumption which explains why it has been so difficult for them to settle their differences with their colonies. The assumption cannot, however, be dismissed as mere nationalistic pride, any more than one can dismiss on the same grounds the pretensions of Americans and Russians to be speaking on behalf of mankind as a whole. The French had something of importance to say to the world in 1789, just as Russians and Americans have today.

It will be objected that the two ideologies at present striving for the attention of mankind are not really members of the same species and ought not therefore to be compared. It is true that we have on the one hand an ideology based on a doctrine clearly defined by a small élite and shared by the members of an alliance. The definition of this doctrine is so sharp that the alliance itself has sometimes been jeopardized by the demand for orthodoxy. On the other side we have not a body of dogma, but an attitude of mind shared in varying degrees, and in some cases scarcely at all, by the members of a much looser alliance. We must not, however, forget that the ideology which formed, and still influences, the United States, was in origin the ideology of a minority[1] and is defined today, in the last resort, in doctrinal terms.

The great declaration of 1776, "We hold these truths to be self-evident, that all men are created equal...", has drawn to the United States generation after generation of men seeking a country where their

[1] Revolutions conducted by a militant minority always produce dissidents. About the same proportion of people took refuge from the American revolution in 1783 as escaped from the Bolshevik revolution in 1917. These figures are perhaps not strictly comparable, since the Americans who left the United States (1 in 66) were all free to do so, whereas the number of Russians (1 in 60) represents only those who were able to get away.

"unalienable rights . . . life, liberty and the pursuit of happiness" are safeguarded. To become an American citizen involves a mental and emotional commitment, not demanded to the same degree of those who find themselves citizens of other countries. The Russian people have not, by deliberate choice rallied to the banner, "from each according to his ability, to each according to his need", yet in the process of time they have come to feel that their country is different in essence from others, that it represents an attempt to reach a standard of social justice, such as has not been undertaken elsewhere. One may challenge the American to prove that his ideal of individual liberty is fulfilled in modern American society; one may challenge the Russian to prove that Soviet society fulfils the ideal of social justice. At the present date one is likely to have a more rational discussion with the American, whose institutions are much older, than with the Russian, but in the last resort the answer in either case will be based on emotion, or if you will, on faith. On both sides there is the faith that the society in which they believe, and for which their own or previous generations have toiled and suffered, has a message for mankind, not simply for its own members. Proffered to the newly-independent countries and backed by a wealth of power and resources, these messages suggest a solution to their problems more sure and more attractive than the modest aid and protection of United Nations.

Unfortunately, ideology, however universalist in intent, provides a very dangerous background for the conduct of international relations. It is dangerous because it produces a distorted picture of the world.

The picture one retains of one's own society is much better, that of the rival society very much worse, than the reality. Such distortions are particularly dangerous in politics when they are accompanied by moral judgments of a particular society or nation. To categorize countries as "good" or "bad" not only produces an artificial division of the world, it makes it impossible —or at any rate very difficult—to conduct international relations at all. There are plenty of cases in current diplomatic relations where moral judgments have postponed rapprochement to a point where it becomes unthinkable. A further danger in the ideological approach is that the ideology itself becomes a major interest of the state which espouses it. It may be difficult to mobilize the enthusiasm of the public on the ground that the possession of this or that island or city is in the interest of national security; but it is not at all difficult to do so if it can be stated that the islanders or citizens are the victims of communist persecution or capitalist exploitation. It is true that such concepts of human rights have always played some part in the formulation of policy, but they have never had the importance now accorded to them: in the minds of the public, if not of the government, ideas of right and justice have become the very foundation of policy. Unfortunately, it is very much easier to reconcile material interests than to reconcile ideas. Thus it was not too difficult to draw a line separating the national interest of the rival powers in Germany and Korea. The powers might or might not have maintained these lines according as seemed convenient and appropriate; but the propagation of differing ideologies behind them has given them a significance which was never intended in the first place and which stultifies, frustrates and complicates all attempts at modification.

As the ideological struggle has progressed it has been accompanied by an arms race of unprecedented cost and magnitude, so that for the first time in history, mutual annihilation is a probable outcome of hostilities. Hesitating to put this panoply to the test, the great powers tend to retreat further behind the ideological barriers which have been created between them, to conduct in propaganda a battle in which they hesitate to engage with outward weapons.

> Since the external disorder, and extravagant lies,
> The baroque frontiers, the surrealist police;
> What can truth treasure, or heart bless,
> But a narrow strictness?

These lines of W. H. Auden were written at a time when a great nation was prisoner of a cruel ideology. The world is still the prisoner of an ideological struggle, symbolized by a wall which cuts a city into two. If Berlin is truly symbolic of the world, how is it possible that we can talk of "United" Nations? Does not the very nature of the modern ideological state render quite impossible the adjustments and the compromises on which alone an international organization can be built? Would not Penn be justified in concluding that, in spite of all that has been achieved in the promotion of international co-operation, the world is now further away than ever from a solution to the fundamental problem?

IV

THE SANDS ON WHICH PEACE HAS TO BE BUILT

NEARLY 270 years have passed since Penn published his Essay. Humanity's experience during that interval, whether good or bad, has proved the necessity for the kind of co-operation which he advocated; yet our situation is more desperate now than it was in 1693. We have failed. Faced with this failure, and conscious of its probable consequences, there are two things we can do: we can concentrate on our prophetic message and commend to our fellow men a better world which is not yet but which is to be; and we can concentrate on politics, considering the next few steps which might lead us out of the morass. These are not mutually exclusive choices. On the contrary, we must undertake both at once; but we must not imagine that our Utopian dreams are a policy for today nor must we assume that our political schemes are a blueprint for Utopia. If we concentrate for a moment on today's political schemes we shall find ourselves working within a narrow framework formed by the basic attributes of human societies from which it is as hard to escape as it would be to eliminate mortality as a factor in human nature. This is not to suggest that these factors cannot be modified; it is, however, suggested that we cannot totally ignore impersonality, power, sovereignty and the pursuit of interests which are among the attributes common to all human societies.

"Impersonality" is one of the fundamental distinctions between an individual and a society, a distinction of which we have constantly to remind ourselves in view of the tendency of our history books and the daily press to describe states as if they were persons. Persons may build their relationships on love; relations between states should be based on law. Love is not an emotion to which a state can properly lay claim. We must not underestimate the magnanimity which some states have recently shown in their foreign policy nor the remarkable generosity shown by the United States and others in sharing their prosperity with their poorer neighbours. But this is enlightened self-interest and it is in the terms of enlightened self-interest or of international obligation that a government must justify its policy. A state which claims to be acting purely from charitable motives is deceiving itself and doing a disservice to the name of charity. The Society of Friends, being freed from the pursuit of political or economic interests, can with much greater justification claim to be motivated by love; but even for it love is difficult to express corporately and is manifested to the world more by its members than by its committees.

Of all the attributes of states, power is the one which Friends are most tempted to ignore or to condemn. We are so deeply concerned at the modern concentrations of power that we feel that the world would be a much safer place without power of any kind. It is true that these concentrations of power are infinitely greater and more costly than would be needed for keeping the peace if the Great Powers were in agreement, but we have to ask ourselves whether, when that agreement is reached, we wish to eliminate power altogether. Is it not the case that there have been some crises in the post-war period—notably in Congo—due as much to the absence of power as to its exercise? Must there not be in the world of 1962 some sanction at the disposal of UN to restrain aggressors? We may shrink from such a prospect and feel that the power of the vote in the General Assembly would be an adequate substitute for arms. Because Friends have a testimony against votes as well as against arms, it might comfort them to reflect that in many of its organs United Nations follows the Quaker principle of finding the sense of the meeting rather than counting heads;[1] but this procedure has only rarely been used in political questions and it is doubtful whether a member state would in present circumstances accept even an overwhelmingly adverse vote on what it considered a matter of vital interest, if that vote were not backed by power.

We are also tempted to ignore or to belittle the state's function in the promotion of interests, forgetting that all societies, including religious societies, exist for that purpose. This temptation is the greater because the interests which states protect are so often expressed in materialistic or militaristic terms, stressing the commercial aspects of our dwelling and neglecting the Immaculate Conception. I recall the contempt I conceived before the war for British foreign policy which, over the centuries, has expended much blood and treasure to prevent Antwerp from falling into the hands of a major continental power. This seemed to me short-

[1] The constitution of the International Atomic Energy Agency is an example of a complex agreement arrived at without a single vote being called for.

sighted folly until one day in May 1940 the Nazi forces invaded the Netherlands and I realized in a flash that this was a threat not only to our material interests but to the whole fabric of our national life. The Society of Friends also has its Antwerps, or its vital interests which it would be difficult to renounce. If faced with the choice between annihilation and the renunciation of their peace testimony, Friends would probably choose annihilation, secure in the faith that the peace testimony would survive by God's good grace. This faith would mitigate for them the cruelty of the choice they had to make. How much more cruel must the choice appear to those—such as the Tibetans—who do not have this consolation!

The pursuit of interests such as these leads states to insist on their sovereignty which gives them the right to identify their interests and determine the means for their protection. The numerous international conventions and institutions already referred to, by harmonizing the interests of the different states which adhere to them, place a voluntary limitation on the exercise of sovereignty. Such limitations may go to considerable lengths, but they are unlikely in present circumstances to reach a point where a state voluntarily surrenders its identity.

We are often tempted to condemn states for exhibiting these characteristics and to forget how much we are bound by them ourselves. The world Society of Friends is in fact greatly hampered in its activities by the limiting effects of sovereignty and power—indeed if we are honest we must admit that the nations have in some respects been more successful than we have in perfecting the art of international co-operation.

If this is the position of a Society constituted as ours now is, how much more difficult would our situation become if we assumed some of the responsibilities of states? Let us for a moment suppose that the Society of Friends decided to convert itself into a close-knit Quaker community, living its separate existence on some desert island. In imagination this is an attractive prospect until we recall that such islands have good reason to be empty, namely the complete absence of natural resources; but in practice we would have no choice, there being no new Pennsylvania at our disposal. The establishment of a Quaker community in such conditions would require an immense capital investment. This would be of two kinds, human capital in the form of labour and material capital in the form of equipment imported from outside. For the first we should find ourselves somewhat ill-provided, having, I suspect, a superfluity of teachers and an abundance of highly-trained scientists, but a notable shortage of technicians and a complete dearth of peasants. We would therefore have to re-train our membership to perform the new tasks which the community demanded, and in this we would not succeed without a higher degree of discipline and a much greater uniformity of doctrine than we now exhibit. These new standards of Quaker life and practice would have to be defended by the exclusion of evil influences from outside; in other words, we would become less tolerant. As to the importation of capital goods we should have to decide whether we could dispense with some vital piece of equipment if its importation bound us too closely to some other economy of whose principles we disapproved.

Let us, however, assume that these immense initial difficulties are overcome and that, by dint of great self-sacrifice by two generations of Friends, our community begins to prosper. At that point, others, who do not share our views, will wish to settle among us. We shall then require an immigration policy. Shall it be exclusion, or quota, or admission on parole? And how are we to implement any of these policies? Perhaps we shall have developed rich lobster fisheries around our coasts; these will attract poachers from neighbouring islands and will at once bring up the question of our legal rights. If our community remains within the United Kingdom, we shall of course be protected from foreign encroachments by the Royal Navy. But would not this dependence on Her Majesty's protection—a sort of colonial status—deny the full expression of our basic principles? Should we not be moved to declare our sovereign independence? At that moment Meeting for Sufferings would have to solve a completely new set of problems. Relations would have to be established with our neighbours, who might want to presume on the traditional generosity of Friends and expect us to base our foreign policy on "turning the other cheek" but, for the sake of our continued existence and the viability of our economy, and in defence of the interests of our community, we should have to make agreements strictly on the basis of reciprocity and justice. We would, no doubt, conduct our diplomacy with dignity and honour, but we would have to conduct it all the same.

The imagination will supply many other facets to this picture of a possible (I do not say desirable!) future development of our Society. Unfortunately, the picture cannot be dismissed as an idle dream. Many of the problems which we have just faced in imagination arose historically for Friends in Pennsylvania: the problem of maintaining the purity of the Quaker faith, the problem of immigration, the problem of the protection of Quaker interests, the problem of power. We may object that our predecessors who took part in the "Holy Experiment" made many mistakes which we could now avoid, profiting by their experience. But the fact that their solutions were inadequate does not mean that the problems themselves do not exist; nor do noble aims exempt a society from facing them.

At the present date the world contains over 100 states facing problems of this nature. Some of them have long traditions giving them, in their own eyes, a historic mission as respectable as that of the Society of Friends; others are new states creating communities in areas little better provided than the desert island of our imagination, with a population ill-trained for the task and finding itself unexpectedly confronted with the realities of independence. All are sensitive about their sovereignty as an essential instrument for the protection of their interests. This is the unpromising material out of which the institutions of peace have to be built. The task seems insuperable, but we have much experience as a guide to its accomplishment.

It is evident that the international institutions which we now possess have been built on the recognition by states of their mutual common interests. Our primary aim must therefore be to seek a community of interests in solving the problems with which we are now confronted. Experience shows that a dogmatic insistence on a national point of view is incompatible with such a search; it follows that we must seek to eliminate the dogmatic approach and encourage restraint and flexibility in the formulation of policies. This is notably the case in the besetting problem of our time—the ideological conflict between East and West—which, as we have seen, prevents the effective operation of international organizations. In this problem, to which we turn first, there is room for individual initiative in breaking down the barriers of misunderstanding which seem to divide the world into two systems of thought; there are also considerations which we must press upon governments either directly or through the medium of public opinion. But the great exponents of rival ideologies are not alone in proposing doctrinaire solutions to current problems. We must therefore also consider the restraints which should be accepted by the uncommitted states in order to strengthen United Nations and to enable it to play a more effective role in securing the benefits of peace. When we have completed our consideration of the political steps towards a more peaceful world, we may then turn to consider the role of Friends as a part of the prophetic line; in other words, we shall first ponder the duties of Hazael and Jehu and turn finally to those of Elisha.

V

EAST v. WEST v. THE REST

UNITED NATIONS was established in 1945 in the expectation, or at least the hope, that the wartime allies would remain united in the pursuit of peace. That expectation has not been fulfilled. It would be wrong to attribute all UN's difficulties to the conflict between East and West, but many of its major problems have arisen from that source. To cite only one example out of many, the prolonged exclusion of the Chinese People's Republic from the "concert" of nations, a direct result of the East-West conflict, has its repercussions in fields from which political questions of this kind are remote: the World Meteorological Organization, for instance, has been unable to include mainland China in its operations, a very serious handicap in the International Geophysical Year; the ILO has had to adopt the fiction that the island of Formosa is one of the ten states "of chief industrial importance"; and control of narcotics cannot be complete without the participation of one of the principal interested parties. How much more damaging is the exclusion of Peking from discussion of so vital a question as disarmament! It must be emphasized that discussions of these subjects would be more realistic if they included the representatives of the largest nation on earth; it does not follow that they would be any smoother. The inclusion of the Chinese People's Republic would in fact serve to emphasize the sharp differences of view between

Marxist and non-Marxist which have been a permanent feature of the life of United Nations. It could be argued that these differences are not completely sterile, that without them important developments, political, economic and social, would not have taken place, and United Nations itself would have been a much less interesting institution. But this is highly speculative. The tragedy for United Nations is that the thesis and antithesis of debate has produced no synthesis, for the good reason that the two sides have been seeking support rather than agreement, using the international forum as an arena for the power struggle. The world can no longer afford to watch two heavily armed camps pursuing their quarrel and in the process making havoc of such machinery as exists for maintaining the peace. It follows that the reduction of the tension between East and West remains the dominant problem of today.

The necessary reduction of the present East-West tension is primarily a matter for the governments concerned, but this does not mean that the dialogue between ordinary citizens of East and West is of no significance. It is admittedly difficult to prove that this dialogue will have any positive or decisive effect on the formulation of policy; but its absence, leading to profound mutual ignorance, will have a negative effect that might well prove decisive at a moment of crisis. At the very least we can expect the dialogue at the personal level to remove the barriers of misunderstanding and misinformation and thus to make war less likely. Furthermore, if we have a political message we cannot expect that we shall find frequent opportunities to deliver it to those in authority, and we must be content to sow its seeds in such soil as may be available. It is therefore not inappropriate that our search for the means of reducing East-West tension should start from a consideration of the relationships between individuals and of the steps we can take to promote and improve them.

We are now well aware of the many barriers to understanding at the personal level. It is one thing to meet and to talk with citizens of the socialist states, but quite another matter to arrive at a meeting of minds; too often our dialogue is a "dialogue of the deaf". Too often the rules of the debate seem to be weighted in favour of the representatives of the socialist states who criticize western policies and institutions with a freedom which they deny to us; too often we have to listen to dreary expositions of the "party line". We have, however, to remember that East Europeans have passed through a period of storm, stress and travail more exacting than anything we have had to suffer; for many of them the Marxist dogma has provided a shelter from the stormy blast of history. We should not be surprised if they are reluctant to venture far outside it. We shall only increase this reluctance if we exhibit impatience or adopt similar tactics by repeating a party line of our own. Happily there is an increasing number of topics on which a discussion can be maintained more or less free from the irrelevant intrusions of political doctrine.

Among these topics pride of place can now be given to Christianity and the Church. Only a little over ten years ago serious communication between Christians of East and West was virtually non-existent. Progress has been slow, but it has been as fast as political conditions have permitted, the Christians of the East having taken advantage of each new relaxation to improve their contacts with the West. The fact that Eastern Christians have only moved as fast as their governments would permit has led many Westerners to dismiss them as being so subservient to political control as to be little better than governmental tools, a point of view which gains support from some of the pronouncements which Eastern Christians feel called to make on international questions. It may appear to Western Christians that their Eastern brethren, when they discuss international peace, are talking the language of the Kremlin; it is important that Western Christians should correct what they feel to be errors of fact in such pronouncements, but it is even more important that their own statements should not talk the language of NATO. The Church must not be identified with either side in the ideological struggle, for the two forms of society now in conflict resemble one another much more closely than either resembles an ideal Christian community. This is a point on which Western Christians, who enjoy a great measure of independence, are free to insist. By God's grace they now have an opportunity of doing so before Eastern Christians within the fellowship of the World Council of Churches.

Other points of contact between East and West are less complicated by questions of fundamental belief. There is indeed one form of religion, the religion of science, of which both sides are equally devoted adherents. It is therefore not surprising that meetings between American and Russian scientists have yielded more positive and important results than any other form of contact. The first United Nations Conference on the Peaceful Uses of Atomic Energy, held at Geneva in 1955, broke down the walls of secrecy which had hitherto surrounded nuclear science and led to a competition in the sharing of information, a process which made an important contribution to the relaxation of tension. More remarkable still have been the series of meetings organized under the name of Pugwash, which have on occasion exercised an influence on political questions, largely because of the high esteem in which scientists are held in the Soviet Union. It is important to remove the last vestiges of suspicion which may attach to Western scientists participating in such discussions. It is also important that scientists should endeavour to break through another wall of secrecy, that surrounding the exploration of space. The fact that the exploration of space has occurred as a result of the development of weapons does not mean that it, any more than atomic energy, must remain a divided science; in fact, it cannot yield the scientific facts which we have a right to expect from so remarkable a development unless it becomes the joint enterprise of all. Even when the exploration of space becomes a co-operative human enterprise instead of a wasteful competition between the two major powers, the scientists will still have the task of advising on whether the enterprise should be undertaken at all at this juncture. Are there not other, earthbound, problems which call more urgently for scientific study and solution, to which the available resources might more properly be devoted? The question is a difficult one since the present needs of humanity require that all the resources of science be focused upon them; yet to insist upon this may interfere with the free development of scientific enquiry. We do not yet possess a body competent to pronounce on this question, but it is one in which United Nations may soon become involved.[1]

A branch of science hitherto supposed to be beyond the pale of fruitful East-West discussion—economics—has recently emerged as one in which there is more common ground than is usually supposed. The fact that economists representing the two "systems" have recently been able to agree on aspects of such an important matter as the economic effects of disarmament, is one of the most hopeful developments of recent years, promising an end to the dogmatism which has hitherto stultified the discussion of economic questions.

A religious society does not have any direct part to play in the discussion of science or economics, but there are two other discussions to which Friends may have a contribution to make. The first of these is the question of semantics. All words tend to be robbed of their original meaning in the process of time, but the process may be more rapid in one area than in another. Thus the word "reactionary", which had a limited and precise significance, has become in the Soviet vocabulary a synonym of "opponent"; at one time the word "bandit" suffered similar treatment in the West. This is regrettable, because it impoverishes polite language and adds to the vocabulary of abuse; but such words as "democracy" and "democratic" have been much more harshly treated, being used on either side to describe

[1] The forthcoming UN Conference on the Application of Science and Technology for the Benefit of the Less Developed Areas will not be able to decide the question of principle, but it may focus attention on questions nearer to human welfare than the moon.

two quite different concepts: in the West the process of counting heads to arrive at a majority opinion, in the East the interpretation of the public weal by an élite. There are many other words and concepts which have acquired double and contradictory meanings. The continued use of the same words to describe such different ideas creates a dangerous thin ice of agreement over a deep morass of incomprehension. The clarification of such issues will be tough, and may seem to damage such harmony as has already been created, but the attempt must be made for the sake of honesty and for the sake of reaching an appreciation of different concepts of right and wrong. This will not result in agreement, but it will transfer the tension from the sterile arena of power to the more fruitful field of ideas.

The second point at which a contribution may still be required from Friends is in breaking down the assumption that the institutions of the socialist states are automatically condemned by virtue of their Marxist origin. The sputnik and Major Gagarin have already broken down Western reluctance to recognize Soviet material achievements. But this is not a great step forward: one ought to expect a materialist philosophy to achieve material successes. What is more difficult to accept is the fact that in quite different fields—child welfare, treatment of offenders, concepts of culture—this same philosophy has also positive achievements to its credit. The study of the ethics of Soviet society may well begin by being a one-way street in which we are the students, they the teachers, but it should lead us to a point where they and we start to travel the same road in search of better forms of society, which neither of the current ideologies has yet shown itself capable of creating.

If such vistas open up it is due to the fact that much effort has been expended on the promotion of personal contacts between East and West. Far be it from us to claim the credit for this progress, but let us be grateful that we have been able to play a humble part in it. And then let us recognize that the whole task has to be undertaken all over again, from the very beginning, with the Chinese, whose present isolation from most of the rest of mankind is far more dangerous than was the isolation of the Russians a decade ago. This task is complicated by circumstances of history and culture, which make personal contact with the Chinese a more expert matter than it is with Europeans. It is unfortunate that so many of those best equipped to converse with the Chinese are debarred from doing so, either by artificial and absurd political barriers, or by prejudices of their own creation. The political barriers create special difficulties for personal contact, since there is evidence that the Chinese themselves will not entertain personal relations until political relations become normal. This reverses the procedure that we find proper in such circumstances and faces us with the possibility of having to wait indefinitely for the political sky to clear before we can pursue what we believe to be the right course. It may well turn out that we have to do this; but we should not abandon the attempt to get into touch simply because it appears to be politically difficult.

If we undertake with the Chinese a similar programme to that which has been pursued elsewhere, we must remember the lessons of our previous experience. We must remember that the attempt will be misunderstood at home, and in certain quarters, especially transatlantic ones, may be regarded as a betrayal. We must remember that there will be disappointments and frustrations as there were with the early contacts with the Russians. We must remember that our first efforts may seem to increase rather than to diminish misunderstanding by revealing the true width of the gulf. These difficulties form a sort of "sound barrier" which has to be broken through. We must also remember that, important though it is to establish ecumenical relations, this does not have in China the same significance as it does in the socialist states of Europe, where Christianity is part of the fabric of national life. Chinese Christians have made an important contribution to the national life, but they remain a tiny minority somewhat apart from the mainstream of Chinese history. For this reason, priority should be given to increasing the scientific relations between China and the West, for in China as in the Soviet Union the scientist plays a vital role in society and his interests should take no account of ideological frontiers. As has already been pointed out, science is not a sphere in which a religious society, as such, has special competence; but if it should prove that science is the way to the hearts and minds of the Chinese, it would not be inappropriate for Friends to open up that way for others.

If we succeed in deepening our relations with the Russians and other East Europeans, and in establishing relations with the Chinese, our discussions with them will not be confined to questions of religious, scientific or cultural interest; they are certain to extend to international affairs, and it is probable that they, not we, will be the first to raise this subject. This is our opportunity to explain to them the attitudes which we feel that governments should adopt in order to strengthen the institutions of peace. There will be many points of disagreement, but we shall be assured of a sympathetic hearing if we can make it clear that we have spoken in exactly the same terms to the West.

One of the first points on which we may—or may not, according to the prevailing orthodoxy—find ourselves in disagreement with them is the question of the inevitability of armed conflict between East and West. The present antagonism between the United States and the Soviet Union is not the first to endanger world peace and differs from its predecessors only in the gravity of its possible consequences. We must insist that these consequences are not inevitable and that the antagonism can be ended, as previous ones have been, by the mutual recognition of common interests. Other quarrels have been terminated in the same fashion as that between tweedledum and tweedledee, by the realization of both contestants that they had more to fear from a third party than from one another. There is no "monstrous crow" in the shape of a third power to make the two great powers of today forget their quarrel, but there are problems of sufficient gravity to compel them to do so, problems in whose solution they have a common interest more compelling than their ideological differences.

The first of these problems is that of the uncommitted third of the world, which consists for the most part of countries in the early stages of development. The outstanding feature of this problem is that we can forecast with reasonable accuracy how it will develop over the next four decades. We know that by the end of this century the present world population will have doubled and that the bulk of this increase will occur in the poorer countries of Asia, Africa and Latin America. Never before has the future status of the human race been foretold with such scientific accuracy. Had Penn been in possession of these forecasts, he would surely have urged the European princes to unite in the search for solutions to the impending problem. The great powers of today have not been entirely deaf to these warnings, but the kind of attention which they have so far paid shows that they have totally failed to grasp the nature of the problem. They have indeed responded to the needs of the developing countries, though not on the scale which the needs demand; the limited size of their response is, however, much less serious than the fact that they have shown more interest in aid as a cold war weapon than in aid for its own sake.

This competitive attitude to world economic development is an insult to human intelligence. To use the needs of others as a means to court favour is to court disaster. Fortunately, there are indications that the developing countries themselves will not permit the wealthier countries to continue to make political capital out of their economic predicament, or to infringe their sovereignty by offering aid on condition of accepting a particular ideological alignment. The newly-independent countries of Africa, for instance, have already shown considerable resentment at the prospect of being the object of a second scramble so soon after emancipating themselves from the results of the first. Fortunately, too, the great powers themselves have so frequently announced their concern for the developing countries, that they cannot afford to offend or neglect them. It remains for them to recognize that it is in their common interest to supply the aid that is required through channels acceptable to the developing countries, namely, through multilateral institutions in which the recipients themselves can state their needs and help to determine the means by which they are met. The multilateral institutions which United Nations has at its disposal for administering economic aid are far from perfect—they might, for instance, benefit by adopting some of the flexibility of the Colombo plan—but they are there to be used and improved by the powers that created them.

To suggest that the United States and the Soviet Union should pool their resources for the benefit of the developing countries is not to suggest that they should suddenly be motivated by disinterested charity. It is in their common political interest to maintain the so-called "third force" as a factor in world politics. It is not, and never has been, in the true interests of great powers so to extend their alliances or blocks that no state is left outside them.[1] This procedure would at once deprive them of the services of neutral intermediaries, upon which in practice they are

[1] The danger was already foreseen in the 18th century when the great powers were indulging in aggrandisement at the expense of the weak, each power requiring territorial "compensation" for the gains of its rivals. It was Choiseul, the French Minister of Foreign Affairs, who, seeing the rapid diminution of territory available for this purpose, asked the pertinent question: "How is compensation to be given for Constantinople?"

constantly calling,[1] and would bring the frontiers of their power into dangerous juxtaposition. The strength of the great powers today is such that it demands a very large number of strong neutrals to maintain the balance between them. It is claimed by the socialist states that the addition of one of the uncommitted nations to their camp is an addition to the forces of peace. This is not so: it is a contribution to the increase of tension and the same would be true of a similar addition to the other side. There is indeed plenty of evidence that the present alliances have reached the limits of manageable size, and it would be in the interests of both to recognize this fact.

The strengthening of the uncommitted nations thus has political as well as economic aspects. The political role which these nations should be enabled to play is closely related to another vital common interest of the great powers: the avoidance of nuclear war. This is loudly proclaimed already as the interest of each side and has been tacitly recognized, for example at the time of the Suez crisis, as a common interest. It is not, however, sufficient that a common interest should be recognized only in times of crisis; it will only bear fruit if it is recognized and pursued constantly. This requires the abandonment of certain façades, such as pretence of each side that it alone is interested in peace, or the assumption that there remain certain problems which only war can solve. But a common interest does not simply imply a common attitude of mind; it also requires common action. The interest in the avoidance

[1] For example, the services of India in Korea and Laos, of many uncommitted nations in Congo, and the constant assumption by Switzerland of diplomatic duties on behalf of others.

of war requires that very urgent common action be taken to prevent war breaking out by accident, which is at present a serious possibility. A good deal of expert study has been given to this problem[1] and this indicates the kind of control measures which the great powers could undertake once they recognize the need and cease insisting that the system either must be perfect or constitutes espionage, both of which exaggerated postures have so far prevented agreement.

An attempt to discuss the problem of surprise attack concurrently with the problem of nuclear tests failed in 1958 and it may be that two problems of this nature are beyond the diplomatic resources of the great powers to tackle simultaneously. If this is so, they may have to choose between the relatively new problem of accidental war and the well-worn one of the discontinuance of nuclear tests as the point at which to begin the active promotion of their common interest. At the time of writing the problem of nuclear tests does not promise further fruitful negotiation. This is tragic. The present impasse is due to the failure first of the USA and then of the USSR to seize the opportunity offered by a genuine and fully recognized common interest, in a limited field, as a subject for negotiation. The early indecision of the United States was due to its inability to reconcile conflicting American opinions on the necessity of a treaty; later the Soviet Union lost interest, presumably as a result of similar internal conflict, though the forces at work are in its case less easily identifiable. To re-vitalize these important

[1] So far, largely by American students. This is a branch of science to which the Soviet Union has given too little attention.

negotiations would require a delicate operation like that undertaken by the servant of Naaman when he persuaded his master to abandon theatrical attitudes and carry out the simple instructions of Elisha.[1] Naaman could do this without serious loss of face; a retreat on the part of the Soviet Union from its present position would involve considerable loss of face,[2] unless it could be masked as a great Soviet concession in the cause of peace, which means that it must not be claimed as a Western victory—for victory is not part of the vocabulary of serious diplomacy. The retreat demanded in this case is a considerable one, since it implies the abandonment, for the time being, of the demand for general and complete disarmament and the acceptance of the small step as the necessary preliminary to wider agreement—accepting Jordan rather than hankering after Abana and Pharpar. Such a retreat can only be made acceptable if it is coupled with a guarantee that the small step is truly a preliminary, and that the interest of either side in disarmament does not end at that point.

In suggesting that the great powers—in particular the two greatest—should recognize this amount of common interest, one is in fact demanding a considerable sacrifice, the abandonment of the notion of victory. The sacrifice is the greater because it has nothing but common sense to recommend it. The logical necessity of abandoning the idea of victory has

---

[1] II Kings 5, 11-14.
[2] The fact that the acceptance by either side of a good idea, put forward by the other, constitutes a loss of face is a modern substitute for the notions of precedency which bedevilled diplomatic negotiation in Penn's day.

already been suggested in relation to aid to newly-developing countries; for common action by capitalists and marxists on their behalf involves the recognition of the fact that neither free enterprise nor communism, in their pure forms, provides an economic panacea. Experience has already shown that one of the hindrances to economic development has been the presentation to newly-developing nations of a simple choice between capitalism and communism, as if these were the only two possibilities or were themselves fixed and immutable alternatives. In fact there are many different solutions to the problem of economic development and there are many indications that the supposedly incompatible economic systems of East and West are changing all the time and growing nearer to one another in the process. It follows that the pursuit of victory on behalf of a particular economic system is out of date. The same holds true of political systems. Our political objective should be a synthesis, combining the Eastern search for social justice with the Western stress on the liberty and dignity of the individual, and achieving a victory for both which would be a triumph for neither.

A second and much more compelling reason to abandon the idea of victory is that victory would be fatal to the ideology itself. If the only way to victory lies through war, then the ideology will perish with its adherents; and neither social justice nor individual liberty will have any further meaning. If it is supposed —and this is a very dubious supposition—that victory can be obtained without war, then, too, the ideology is doomed: for Marxism, as soon as it becomes a universal orthodoxy, will fall by its own weight, having nothing further against which to struggle; while the ideals of the West could not achieve universal success in the immediate future without employing stratagems incompatible with their true spirit. The notion of victory is thus not in the real interests of the ideals and aspirations which the two sides proclaim.

Such conclusions are, however, very hard to accept. Government requires a moral sanction to justify its continued existence, and loyalty to an ideology provides this sanction, replacing the Divine Right or the "Mandate of Heaven" of former times; but if these ideologies are deemed to be of universal validity, how is it possible to abandon the struggle for their universal acceptance and still retain the "mandate of heaven"? Such a retreat from cherished and long-proclaimed aims requires the abandonment by the leaders of the socialist states of their role as the high priests of Marxism and a return to the more modest function of government which is to pursue "the art of the possible". Their problem is that the totalitarian system which they have created has destroyed any independent, non-governmental institutions to which they could entrust the ideological flame. Without this flame it might not be possible to maintain the tempo of progress, and the bonds of society would be loosened. There is, however, plenty of evidence that the average Soviet citizen is beginning to be critical of the ambitious projects of his leaders, so that the flame has lost its power; in other countries where the socialist system is still in its early youth—notably in China—the prospect of world revolution continues to be a consolation for present-day hardships and to be proclaimed with an intransigence directly related to the domestic uncertainties of the régime.[1] It follows that the consolidation of the present régimes in the socialist states would be in the interests of peace rather than otherwise.

The situation in the West is almost the reverse. Instead of the government using ideology as a stimulus to the efforts of its citizens, the citizens use it to stimulate the ardour of the government which tries to pursue the "art of the possible" by restraining the misplaced enthusiasm of the electorate. Thus, the abandonment of the notion of victory involves for the governments of the West a smaller sacrifice than it does for those of the East; but the sacrifice demanded from the people is very much greater, requiring that they abate their crusading zeal. We look forward to the time when the Russians and the Chinese are prepared to pay only lip-service to the idea of a total victory for their system; this time will come only if we can persuade the average American citizen to abandon his ready classification of régimes into the "good" and the "bad", to admit the possibility of American aid to societies with a socialist economy, and to accept that, for this generation, life and the pursuit of happiness cannot invariably be accompanied by liberty.

We have faced governments and peoples with a grave dilemma and it is only fair that we should now face our own. We have suggested that governments should no longer seek the immediate achievement of those ideological aims which seem to give a moral sanction to national policy; yet, stripped of the com-

[1] This does not apply solely to the socialist states; one can think of several western governments whose intransigence is directly related to their weakness.

plexities of power, these are noble aims. We have suggested, in short, that governments become less idealistic and forfeit some of the moral sanction which gives them authority. Is it reasonable for us to ask that they should then adopt a new idealism based on the highest standards of Christian behaviour? How moral, how idealistic, do we expect a government to be? If we are thinking in terms of today we have to ask ourselves whether the noblest aspirations of Christian pacifism, if adopted as governmental policy, could survive untarnished the pressures of power or avoid degenerating into dogmatism. The question can only be answered according to conviction and the answer to which the present thesis leads may well be wrong. It seems to me, however, that in present conditions we ought not to expect that governments will suddenly be led to behave towards one another in accordance with our interpretation of Christian morality. What we may expect is that they devote themselves to the task of building institutions for the peaceful settlement of disputes, in which they can co-operate together in meeting the urgent needs of mankind. This task will be difficult and sometimes sordid, involving long negotiation and hard bargaining; the resulting conception will certainly not be immaculate. This is a humbler role than governments have chosen for themselves and its moral sanction must derive not from nations or from parties, but from those human aspirations whose fuller realization the institutions of peace must be designed to serve.

VI

THE DILEMMAS OF INTERNATIONAL CO-OPERATION

WE have considered some of the sacrifices which have to be made by both sides in order to achieve a measure of understanding between East and West, sacrifices requiring from both government and people a profound mental and spiritual adjustment. It would, however, be unjust and unrealistic to suppose that the East-West conflict is the sole cause of current world tensions and that the rest of the world has nothing to do but wait in patience or suspense for the great powers to come to terms. In fact, the reduction of East-West tensions will not be possible unless other nations take positive action to promote an atmosphere favourable to *détente*. This has not been achieved in the past 15 years. Recent failures to arrive at a rapprochement can be attributed in part to direct conflicts between the great powers over such matters as the U-2 incident and Berlin, but they can also be attributed in even larger measure to events in Congo which did not originate in the East-West conflict but exacerbated that conflict, especially when Congolese politicians invited the intervention of external forces for the solution of internal problems.

The relation of internal problems to the problem of East-West rapprochement has recently been illustrated by events in Laos where a situation endangering international peace arose as a result of the intervention of both East and West in the internal affairs of the country. After seven months of negotiation the powers have reached an agreement on the methods of securing international respect for the neutrality of Laos, a commendable achievement resulting from the common interest of both sides in avoiding conflict and the realization that this interest can only be secured by mutual concessions. But the agreement will not be a lasting one unless Laotian politicians recognize their duty to refrain from appealing for support to one side or the other in the ideological conflict. If they neglect this duty the powers will be tempted to put supposed national interest before international responsibility, and the agreement will be endangered. No state can continue to enjoy the privileges of neutral status without incurring obligations which constitute a limitation on its sovereign freedom of action.[1] An uncommitted nation is not in all respects freer than a member of an alliance; its commitments are different. Unless a commitment to the obligations of neutrality is included among their engagements, the uncommitted nations will not be able to play the mediating role to which they aspire.

To demand the acceptance of such commitments from the leaders of newly-independent countries is to demand a great deal, for they are struggling to carry out simultaneously three revolutions, social, economic

---

[1] Newly-independent countries are very reluctant to accept binding limitations on a sovereignty which they have so recently acquired. Similar hesitation is shown by dictatorial régimes. The development of international legality will depend very much on the development of national or internal legality.

and political, against a background of grinding poverty and often of hidebound tradition. These are compelling national problems which appear to demand a quick, short-term solution. Among such solutions is the policy of reaping the benefits of the cold war. That there are real, short-term benefits to be reaped has been shown most recently by the experience of India whose forceful annexation of Goa was possible because it was known beforehand that on this issue the Security Council would not be united in defence of Article 2(4) of the Charter which binds Member States "to refrain in their international relations from the threat or use of force". India's experience is not unique; one can also cite, for instance, Egypt's successful defiance of the Security Council in the matter of permitting Israeli ships to use the Suez Canal. Economically, too, the cold war may have been advantageous to the newly-independent countries who, by displaying the aid received from one side, have been able to encourage a further contribution from the other. Unfortunately, they have some reason to doubt whether they would have received so much aid had the USA and the USSR been allies instead of antagonists. It would, however, be short-sighted policy on the part of the newly-independent countries to seek the continuation of the cold war simply because of the aid which may be obtainable by playing off one side against the other. It must be remembered that such economic benefits as may have resulted are only a small fraction of the cost of the cold war and that to promote the cold war for the sake of these marginal profits is to condemn the world to a wasteful use of its resources—and possibly to early extinction.

The temptations to which newly-independent countries sometimes succumb when seeking a solution to their problems may account for the frequent use of the word "irresponsible" to describe their policies. The word is not justified if it simply means that they do not cast their votes in the General Assembly on the "right" side. Western powers who have enjoyed majority support for so long must grow accustomed to finding themselves outvoted, a salutary and chastening experience which is more a comment on their own actions than a proof that United Nations has failed. Nor is it fair to define "irresponsibility" in terms of limitation of outlook. The current crusade against the remaining outposts of colonialism may display a limited outlook, but can it be shown that the establishment of colonialism, with its "baroque frontiers" cutting across tribal divisions, showed a great breadth of view on the part of today's "responsible" powers? Unfortunately, the best that can be claimed is that the division of Africa showed great responsibility towards the need to keep the peace in Europe and total irresponsibility towards the non-European races who paid the price.[1]

Only in one respect can the newly-independent countries properly be described as "irresponsible". The changes which they seek to effect may be just and desirable, but they are changes for which, in the last resort, others will pay, whether in terms of cash, or concessions. This situation is not the fault of the newly-

[1] Poland in the 18th century similarly paid the price of peace between the great powers, presenting Europe with a problem which was not solved for over a century. Only Maria Theresa of Austria recognized the immorality of the "responsible action" in which she took part— "she wept but she took her share".

independent countries, but it does impose upon them the responsibility to respect the intentions and the susceptibilities of those who will ultimately have to bear the cost. There may be times when they must choose between their need for peace and their desire for change.

The desire for change brings us face to face with a problem that has not yet been solved and to which the founders of international organizations have given too little attention. Hitherto, in the last resort, war has been the vehicle of change; if war is abolished, how is change to be effected? Neither Penn's proposal, nor the similar one pressed upon the Powers at the Congress of Utrecht by the Abbé de St. Pierre, made provision for peaceful change. What would have happened had these plans been adopted? It is possible that a European Diet might have provided Frederick the Great with some alternative to war as a means of satisfying his "ambition, self-interest and the desire to make people talk of me";[1] it is possible that it might, like the Pope in 1494, have drawn a line to separate the rival colonial ambitions of the English and the French; but how would it have dealt with the French Revolution? This is not an academic question; it is directly relevant to UN's present predicament. Attempts made in the past to establish an international order have been linked to the maintenance of a *status quo* defined by treaty—Vienna in 1815, Versailles in 1919; Penn himself suggested that his Diet should define the *status quo* in the terms of the Treaty of Nijmwegen of 1678. The assumption that a particular

[1] His self-confessed reasons for going to war in 1740.

treaty should be regarded as final is, of course, satisfactory only to those who, having emerged victorious, feel that they have few further ambitions. An organization closely linked to a treaty will maintain itself only if it is given power to modify the treaty or so long as the treaty commands general support in its original form. As soon as there is a power—especially a revolutionary power—prepared to challenge the treaty settlement, the organization itself will be in danger. Neither the Holy Alliance nor the League of Nations survived this danger.

United Nations is at an advantage compared with its predecessors in being linked to no treaty settlement —indeed, throughout its existence so far there has not been an over-all *status quo* for it to defend. The two greatest of the powers which emerged victorious from the Second World War, being both revolutionary powers and new to the responsibilities of great power status,[1] cannot be described as satisfied or conservative powers in the sense that this was true of the leaders of the League of Nations, since both wished to proceed from victory to remould the world according to their own conceptions of justice. The United States, which raised the anti-colonial banner long before the Soviet Union was born, enjoying the support of the great majority of members in the early days of United Nations, has tended to regard that body as an instrument for implementing its world policy. The Soviet Union has up to the present been so consistently in a minority that it is remarkable that she should have

[1] It is not intended to imply that neither the USA nor the USSR was a great power before the war, but from 1919 to 1941 neither played in world affairs the role to which its importance entitled it.

remained a member for so long. She has, however, found compensation for her isolation, as Britain did for her dissatisfaction with the Holy Alliance, by calling into existence a new world to redress the balance of the old; and she has done so by methods which have shaken, though not destroyed, the foundations of the organization to which she continues to belong. So far from defending the *status quo*, United Nations has been the witness of, and in many cases has given sanction to, momentous changes in the world map. The question which the organization now has to face is whether it is not just as dangerous to be the promoter of change as it was for the Holy Alliance and the League to attempt to defend the *status quo*.

If we consider the (perhaps extreme) case of Goa as an example of the changes which have taken place, we have to recognize, first, that it would not have occurred as it did had United Nations really been united; and, secondly, that an infringement of Article 2(4) of the Charter has been justified on the ground that the change thereby accomplished was in conformity with a General Assembly resolution against colonialism. Evidently, even violent changes can be justified by reference to "world public opinion" as expressed by votes in the General Assembly. In the case of Goa one vital element in world opinion was missing, namely Portuguese opinion. If it is objected that Portuguese opinion is too benighted to count, then United Nations loses its claim to be a defence of the weak against the strong. Had there been in Portugal, as there is in Britain, a strong movement in favour of colonial emancipation, the situation might have been quite different; but such a movement is only in its infancy, and most Portuguese still seem to cherish as valid the colonial mission bequeathed to them by Vasco da Gama. Such attitudes, however outmoded they may be, cannot be changed by votes in the General Assembly; indeed, it is debatable, after the long experience with South Africa, whether the discussion of questions of domestic jurisdiction by the General Assembly does more to promote or to retard a change of heart. We must conclude that a political instrument like United Nations[1] does not have a primary role to play in bringing about changes which have to come from within; in South Africa results are more likely, in present circumstances, to come from the action of the World Council of Churches and the Vatican than from any number of resolutions voted at New York.

This faces United Nations, and especially its younger members, with a serious dilemma. The principle of non-intervention in internal affairs, which has been written into the UN Charter, has a respectable ancestry, having originally been a protection against the interference of reactionaries; but our experience with Nazi Germany has revealed the extent to which questions of domestic jurisdiction may become questions of international concern. It is thus not difficult to argue that the policy of *apartheid* may similarly one day, and sooner rather than later, produce a threat to world peace, and that it is, in consequence, already a matter of international concern. It is, however, doubtful whether these conclusions, which result from natural impulses, are compatible with the con-

[1] Another political instrument, the Commonwealth, has also failed to promote any noteworthy change in South Africa's internal policy.

tinued existence of United Nations as an association of sovereign states. It may be permissible for states to express their righteous, or self-righteous, indignation at conditions obtaining in their neighbour's territory, but the line between indignation and intervention is a narrow one and, once it is crossed, United Nations confronts dangers which may well prove fatal. This is not to argue that changes are not necessary, or that the policy of *apartheid* is fully in accord with the principles of the Charter; it is not, any more than is slavery, though the two Member States where this institution remains legal have not, so far, been the target of frequent or violent criticism. Of course, change must occur—for we cannot enjoy true peace so long as colonialism, *apartheid* and slavery persist—but it should be brought about not by violence, nor even by votes, but by the operation of spiritual forces which can best flourish in an atmosphere of political restraint.

The frequent discussion by the General Assembly of questions of domestic jurisdiction tends to obscure the primary function of United Nations which is to serve as a medium for the settlement of international disputes. We need not insist that it be the only such medium in order to establish its authority and prestige, for the world has need for a variety of methods of keeping the peace and it certainly has need of a United Nations endowed with as strong and effective a mechanism as its members are prepared to entrust to it.

To ensure respect for the law it is necessary to have some ultimate sanction for its enforcement. At present, international law is not an exception to this rule, but the ultimate sanction does not exist. The creation of an international police force to serve this purpose is as yet not a practical possibility, but it should be the objective of the forthcoming disarmament discussions. Meanwhile, an effective sanction hangs by the slender thread of agreement between the United States and the Soviet Union, whom no lawbreaker can resist if they decide to act in unison. It might be supposed that if these two powers could be persuaded to act in unison there would be no further need for United Nations; but the direct domination of the world by the two super-powers would in practice be intolerable without an organization to direct and approve the use of their power. Furthermore, as experience at the time of the Suez crisis showed, their power is best exercised at a distance and through a neutral medium. For this reason alone, the machinery of United Nations will continue to be essential for the maintenance of the peace, even if the necessary condition of an East-West understanding is secured.

In the absence of that understanding, the machinery of United Nations still has an important role to play, especially as an instrument of diplomacy. This function was developed by Dag Hammarskjöld, under whose leadership United Nations contributed to the solution of a number of international crises, all of which would have become a more serious threat to world peace had there not been an independent intermediary to assist in resolving them. The possibility of making use of United Nations in this way should be increased rather than restricted as seems to be the present tendency. There is a great deal to be said for providing UN with a small diplomatic service of its own, consisting of men trained in the profession who would be stationed at important capitals, particularly those in developing areas. This would provide a reserve of the type of individual which has been conspicuously lacking in recent UN operations, the man whose business is in the political rather than in the technical field. Hitherto the demand for political officers has been met either by taking officials from duties more or less remote from the diplomatic functions to which they are called, or by borrowing from the diplomatic corps of the (now very few) "reliable neutrals", or by putting a great strain on the Secretary-General himself. The suggestion that this need be met by additions to the UN Secretariat and to the number of its "members at large" will, no doubt, be opposed chiefly by those who have been loudest in their criticisms of UN's inadequacy in this regard. Criticisms from such sources in the past have, as often as not, been a tribute to the efficacy of the Secretary-General's diplomacy rather than the reverse, since its function has been to curb the ambitions of the powers concerned.

The suggestion that the diplomatic role of United Nations should be strengthened will not be acceptable to those members of the public who conclude from recent experience that the organization has failed. This conclusion is based on a number of false premises. It is, firstly, a mistake to imagine that in present circumstances United Nations could achieve a conspicuous success, providing all its members with a cheap and vicarious victory. Any action that it may undertake can only be based on the "lowest common denominator" of agreement to be found among its members. When this figure is small, as was the case in Congo, the action will be limited in effectiveness and can only achieve the small programme on which the majority is agreed. This is bound to fall a long way short of the maximum aims of each individual nation. But this is also true of any form of diplomatic negotiation, of which all that one is entitled to expect is that the result will be satisfactory.

Behind the complaints about the ineffectiveness of United Nations lurks the feeling that the problems which it has found so hard to solve could easily have been settled by war. This assumes that war provides a clear and decisive answer, whereas in reality it raises more problems than it solves and would undoubtedly, had it been prolonged in Suez or undertaken in Congo, have offered no clearer or more decisive an answer than has been obtained through UN action. The belief in the effectiveness of war is, of course, confined to "limited" wars or "police action", of whose inefficacy, however, ample demonstration has recently been given. The "limited" wars attempted in the post-war years have mostly failed to achieve their objectives because the interests at stake can no longer be confined to those of the parties to the dispute. Any dispute thus becomes everybody's dispute—a fact overlooked by those who hanker after the good old days of the *Pax Britannica*[1]—and as soon as that happens war ceases to be "limited" or to provide the clear and decisive solution expected of it. Today's dilemma arises

---

[1] The correspondent of the *Daily Telegraph* already quoted (see note on p. 23), while vehemently attacking "wishful thinking", proposes that we "revert to the less chaotic pre-League of Nations days". Less chaotic for whom?

from the fact that though war has become useless as an instrument of national policy, our thinking is still based on its supposed efficacy, largely because no alternative instrument has been perfected for settling disputes and legalizing change.

United Nations has not yet provided this alternative, though it is an essential element of any workable one. Consequently, the search for an alternative must include an attempt to improve the mechanism of United Nations and its Agencies. This presents us with a number of dilemmas, even in the field of technical co-operation where there have been considerable achievements. One dilemma arises from the difficulty of co-ordinating programmes undertaken by a number of relatively autonomous Specialized Agencies. Should this autonomy be restricted or should we recognize that the kind of "imperialism" which an institution builds up around its own activities gives it a vigour and sense of purpose which are worth preserving? Is Agency autonomy a way of avoiding excessive international bureaucracy—a disease from which the Agencies themselves suffer—and how can bureaucratic tendencies be avoided in institutions which serve 104 masters? Closely related to the problem of co-ordinating the technical assistance activities of United Nations is that of improving the organs in which economic and social questions are discussed. The Economic and Social Council, like other organs created for a United Nations half its present size, is too small to be truly representative of the membership. Even if enlarged, however, it would not be better able to deal with the immense variety of questions within its competence.

Should some of its functions be delegated to the Regional Economic Commissions, especially those for Africa, Latin America and Asia and the Far East? Should these regional bodies be given greater competence in the discussion of social questions or in the co-ordination of technical assistance in their respective areas?

These questions are directly relevant to the question of keeping the peace since it is of vital importance to improve the institutions at the disposal of United Nations for furnishing technical and economic aid to the newly-independent countries, whose political maturity and stability, so important for United Nations, depend in large measure on their ability to surmount their economic problems. There are plenty of questions more closely related still to UN's peace-making functions. The revision of the Charter, which has already been mentioned in relation to the Economic and Social Council, can be discussed, but discussion will remain academic until the question of Chinese representation is solved. This question, in its turn, requires much careful study, and it must not be supposed that a "simple" (in practice, of course, it is very complex) change in representation will automatically solve a number of problems. It will solve old problems by presenting us with new ones: the China problem will revolve not around mainland China but around Formosa.

Presumably, a change in Chinese representation would be followed by an influx of Chinese members of the Secretariat, most of whom would undoubtedly insist on the rights of Chinese as one of the five official languages of UN. The assimilation of the Chinese into the Secretariat will be a task superimposed on that which has already been undertaken in respect of citizens of other socialist states, of whom there have been far fewer in the Secretariat than a fair distribution would permit. The disparity is now being rectified, but the process will take time. Unfortunately, it will not necessarily increase the efficiency of the Secretariat unless the Soviet Union and its allies abandon a principle and an *arrière pensée*: the principle is that vacancies in the Secretariat should be filled by national civil servants lent for short periods to the international organizations, a principle valid for a limited number of posts but disastrous if universally applied. The *arrière pensée* is that Soviet citizens working in the Secretariat should have a continuing loyalty to the USSR, and not necessarily give their first loyalty to the organization which they serve. This theory was at the basis of the troika proposal which assumed that the three Secretaries-General would represent the views of the different blocs from which they came. If it had been adopted, this proposal would have removed the essential qualities of independence and objectivity from the Secretariat and rendered it less capable of acting effectively in the kind of situation for which the troika was designed. Even without a troika in the full sense of the term it may be necessary to choose between the principle of an independent Secretariat and a Secretariat drawn impartially from all the members; these are not necessarily the same for there are many member states, besides the socialist states, who are hesitant about the principle, and unversed in the practice, of an independent civil service, whether national or international.

The troika proposal originated in Soviet dissatisfaction with what was regarded as the excessive independence of the Secretariat. As a remedy it proposed to destroy that independence altogether by introducing the unacceptable principle of representation into the executive arm of an international organization. This was not its only constitutional implication. The proposal was based on the observation that the world is now divided into three camps. The vigour with which this "political reality" has been stressed has led people to ask whether the constitutions of international organizations should not be adapted to take account of it. Even if we accept the tripartite division of the world as a current fact—though it is a gross over-simplification of the situation—we have to ask whether it is such a durable fact of international life that we are justified in basing constitutions upon it. It is dangerous to assume the immutability of a particular historical situation, as has been shown by the experience of the ILO which started life with a tripartite constitution carefully designed to meet the social situation of 1919; the challenge of socialism to the basis of this constitution has given the ILO several years of crisis. If Penn's proposed constitution had been adopted even greater difficulties would have arisen: he suggested a system of "weighted" votes, giving 12 to Germany, 10 each to France and Spain, 6 to England and smaller numbers to some entities which have now disappeared. One can imagine the lengthy negotiations that would have preceded the acceptance of this allocation of voting strength and the tenacity with which the decisions, once written into the constitution, would have been defended long after they had ceased to bear any relation to "political realities". A constitution carefully written to meet the basic assumption of the troika would, in the course of time, produce similar vested interests in a settlement that was no longer realistic.

National temperament and experience would lead the British to conclude that in these circumstances it would be a great mistake to spell out the constitution of UN in too great detail, claiming that the spirit should have precedence over the letter of the law, and that problems should be solved as they arise not provided for in advance on the basis of some general principle. They would find themselves in a minority for their experience, immensely valuable though it has been, has been conditioned by particular circumstances. The experience of another politically-mature people has been different. The Swiss Federal Constitution legislates for a number of details of the national life which one would not expect to be mentioned in such a document; one gets the impression that the Swiss themselves have in consequence become unduly sensitive about the letter of the law. But this is a natural result of creating a multi-lingual country, since you can only convey the spirit of a law in a language which is fully understood in all its *nuances*. This cannot always be done in Switzerland by word of mouth, so that the written document gains greatly in importance. The more polyglot your institution becomes the more it is bound to express itself in writing, or by the "letter". One of the tasks of those who wish to assure the future of United Nations will therefore be to harmonize the freedom of the spirit with the precision of the letter of the Charter.

BUILDING THE INSTITUTIONS OF PEACE

These are a few of the many problems to be faced as we proceed to build up the institutions of peace. They are difficult problems but they are not insoluble provided there is a positive desire on the part of Member states to find a solution. At the time of writing the future is in doubt. Some states seem to be weary of the attempt to build, others to be reluctant because the building requires that they contribute bricks from their national sovereignty. To abandon now the position we have reached and to permit painfully developed organisms to fall into desuetude would be wanton recklessness in view of the dangers which threaten humanity. It is possible that humanity does not deserve institutions for its advancement and protection because it has not yet learned to think in human terms. Yet, if we must continue to think in purely national terms would it not be better to do so within a world-wide body rather than in "splendid isolation"?

VII

THE SMALL VOICE OF PROPHECY

In the two previous chapters we have considered some of the principles which might render the Hazaels and the Jehus of today more useful servants of the Lord. We now turn in conclusion to consider the duty of a religious society which attempts to continue the prophetic mission of Elisha.

We have to ask ourselves at the outset whether the Society of Friends, or indeed any branch of the Christian Church, has any call to concern itself with the sordid realities of international affairs. Does the Immaculate Conception have any relation whatever to commerce? There are politicians who would answer with a contemptuous "No", in the mistaken belief that morals are totally irrelevant to politics. In this they grossly belittle the nature of their political calling which loses all validity if it abandons the attempt to translate moral principles into practical action. The Christians who tell us that politics are irrelevant to morals are on surer ground, since Christian hope is not founded upon political peace; if it were it could never have survived the 2,000 years of wrong which it has had to endure since it was first proclaimed. We cannot but regret the tribulation, the nakedness, the peril and the sword, but we cannot forget that "in all these things we are more than conquerors through Him that loved us", and that the Christian message is to be proclaimed in all circumstances, even when hell itself seems to have broken loose. Such was the experience of Rendel Harris when, after his ship had been torpedoed in the Mediterranean, he landed with others at Alexandria in a state of "Apostolical one-stage-from-nudity", to be met at the Customs House with the irrelevant, political question, "Have you anything to declare?"; he felt that the only possible answer in the circumstances was, "We declare unto you glad tidings".[1] All too often, the question put to us by politics cannot be answered in any other way.

Yet the Society of Friends, if not always and everywhere at least often and in many of its branches, has declined to interpret the Christian message as a command to stand aside from the affairs of this world or to set itself apart as a chosen people. We have always held that no aspect of human life is beyond the reach of God's mercy, that it is God's purpose to redeem the world and that we are called to serve this purpose to the utmost extent of the guidance that we receive. It is thus our duty to reaffirm our faith that the jungle of international politics is not beyond redemption, that the glad tidings which we declare may yet be reflected in a world which has found the path to peace. Such an affirmation will be dismissed as foolish optimism, but it is the destiny of Christian Hope to be regarded as foolishness, not only by Greeks but by others who imagine that human reason, unsupported by faith, is capable of meeting the challenge of the human condition. That challenge is now so pressing that the mind will abandon the attempt to meet it, if not sustained by the message of prophecy.

[1] Rendel Harris: *Ulysses to his Friends*, p. 14.

The message that we have to deliver, both to the world and to the rulers of it, has its temporal and its eternal aspects. Most of the topics which we have considered so far belong to the realm of time. It is possible that in a few years these problems will seem insignificant, but time alone will not solve them without a positive commitment on our part; nor will their solution absolve us from facing the new crises which the future will bring. These temporal problems may appear remote from the historic peace testimony of the Society of Friends, which belongs to the realm of eternity. This is not so. Who can tell to what extent Man's undoubted progress towards international peace is due to' the prophetic message that such peace is possible? Is it not conceivable that without the intervention of foolish pacifists the wise world might now be rushing to destruction, like lemmings in a year of abundance, unaware of any alternative destination? The peace testimony will continue to give meaning and inspiration to our message for today, and it loses none of its validity if, to the uncompromising negative of our refusal to bear arms, we add a demand for a positive commitment to the international idea.

It is difficult for us to ask this because we ourselves do not find it easy to make such a commitment; it is much easier in present circumstances to see what is wrong and oppose it than to see what is right and support it—perhaps because opposition to wrong belongs to the realm of eternity, support for the right policy to the realm of time. The problem was brought home to me by the question of nuclear tests. Not only the peace movement but a very large section of the public was rightly convinced that it was wrong to

BUILDING THE INSTITUTIONS OF PEACE

conduct nuclear tests, and the resulting wave of moral indignation helped to bring the three nuclear powers to the conference table. But, having once got the conference started, it was more difficult to maintain the same degree of support for the positive action it was taking than it had been to create the uncompromising negative which brought it into being. It was felt, and as it turned out with some justification, that the spontaneity of the movement against tests was being dissipated in a series of dreary discussions over points of detail whose significance was hard to grasp. It is difficult to say whether the outcome would have been different had there been, throughout the conference, as wide a measure of support for its work as there was for the idea it was trying to implement. It is, however, clear to me that the temporal, as distinct from the eternal, function of the peace movement is not merely to work for the elimination of a particular evil but also to co-operate actively in building the institutions which must take its place, as a treaty was to replace tests. This means that when we say "No" to war we must also say "Yes" to United Nations, even though that institution falls far short of embodying Man's noblest aspirations.

To take a hand in the building of institutions is not a task which appeals to all of us, and fortunately so, for there are many other tasks to be performed. Support for the international idea needs a commitment to personal attitudes as well as to organizations. It requires that we shed, and ask others to shed, those national prejudices which make international co-operation so difficult. This cannot be done simply by inverting our prejudices and assuming that every other nation is right and ours alone is wrong. There may be moments when this is actually true—and the international idea demands that we admit our country's faults; it does not demand that we deny or belittle its achievements. Internationalism requires that we contribute what our country has to offer, not that we withhold a contribution because we are too much aware of our country's shortcomings. This principle lies behind the formation of an international civil service whose members are not expected to abstract themselves from their national background, in an attempt to be neutral which only results in their becoming "neuter". They are expected to contribute from the riches of their national traditions to the furtherance of the international cause.

The international cause today also requires from us a possibly unpopular and puritanical message. We are aware of the gulf that separates the prosperous minority from the underfed majority of mankind. The gulf is only deepened when one reads in the same newspaper about famine in Kenya and conflict in Congo and about the latest refinement offered to the ladies of the West: self-adhesive false eyebrows, in three qualities designed to produce a coy, an inviting or a domineering effect. One cannot help recalling the remark attributed to Marie Antoinette when she was told that the people were clamouring for bread: "Cannot they eat cake?"; and the fate that befell the *ancien régime* because it was not sufficiently aware of the conditions of the world about it. Our affluent society can only afford the luxury of false eyebrows if it is truly aware of the world's needs; and if it diligently seeks ways of serving suffering humanity it may find that such fantasies cease to have any appeal. The concept of service is an integral part of the international idea.

The Society of Friends has done much to promote the idea of voluntary international service, especially that form of it first conceived by Pierre Ceresole at the end of the first world war. We need more than ever to encourage the development of skills, including the knowledge of languages, and the spirit of adventure and of self-sacrifice which render such service valuable both to the giver and to the receiver; and we need to seek ways and means of making volunteer service available in the distant areas where it is most needed and of making it the gateway to international service of a more permanent kind. The promotion of various forms of international service will give us an opportunity to co-operate with other groups who, like ourselves, are seeking ways to peace, though their point of departure on this search is different from ours. Similar opportunities are open to us in our attempts to promote international understanding by bringing together in conferences or seminars representatives of different races and nations for the discussion of common problems.[1]

Valuable though this work has been, I suggest that it needs to be supplemented by work for understanding at a deeper level than is possible at a work camp or

[1] Seminars and Conferences, which have been organized by Friends for a number of years, aim to bring together a group of about 35 people as widely representative as possible of the nations of the world. Formal sessions for lectures are reduced to a minimum and their purpose is to stimulate discussion among the participants. Such discussion and the many opportunities offered for personal friendship help to remove prejudice and to open the mind to different patterns of thought. Seminars for students and young professionals may last for three weeks, Conferences for younger diplomats for 10 days.

seminar. It is now relatively easy to obtain a superficial knowledge of a number of countries which air transport has made so much more accessible than they were a generation ago. This has created the illusion that the distances between us are trivial and that the whole world is but an extension of London, or New York or Moscow, whatever our starting point may be. This brings familiarity but not understanding, for understanding requires that we first recognize the distance, both in space and time, that lies between us and another people. I recall that when I was caught in a small Japanese air raid on a town in southern China I came upon a badly wounded man whom I took for shelter to the porch of a nearby house. I was much put out when the lady of the house ordered me to take the man away; it seemed that I had encountered not a human being but a member of a different species. When I recounted this incident with much indignation to a Friend who knew China intimately, he said to me: "Ah! But you do not understand. You could not possibly have done that woman a worse turn than to lay on her doorstep what she took to be a dying man." And he went on to explain that she would not only have been held responsible had the man died—as, alas, seemed all too likely—but would also have been haunted ever after by his spirit. Such concepts, though remote from my own, have an unmistakably human ring; and as soon as I recognized this fact the woman became again a fellow human being.

It should be the goal of understanding to pierce first through the thin layer of superficial familiarity and then through the hard rock of differing customs, habits and beliefs to discover the real humanity that lies beneath. National, racial and religious differences have not destroyed our common humanity, but they have given it different faces which may tempt us to forget that all the things that really matter, life and death, birth and love, joy and sorrow, poetry and prayer, are common to us all. The sense of our common humanity is latent within us, but only occasionally do we appreciate it as a living reality, as when at times of great stress we are upheld by strangers of an alien creed and tongue. Then the inward eye is opened and we see humanity standing above all nations, more humble, more patient and far more enduring than all the kingdoms of this earth. This is the ultimate justification for our peace-making. This provides the mysticism without which any international organization will become perishable nonsense.

It is the sense of the presence of humanity which compels us to convey a message not only to the world, but also to those set in authority, statesmen and politicians, delegates and diplomats, on whom falls the burden of making decisions for today and provision for an unknown tomorrow. We approach the rulers of the world because our faith compels us to do so, and if we are received it is because our faith has earned us respect. What we seek in these approaches is a meeting of minds, such as may have taken place when Mencius went to see King Liang Hui and was greeted with the words: "Honoured Sir, since you have not thought it far to come 1,000 miles, may I assume that you have counsels of profit to my kingdom?"; or when Cromwell turned to Fox and said: "Come again to my house, for if thou and I were but one hour a day together we should be nearer one to the other." If we are so bold as to come again to the house of the great and to attempt to give counsels of profit we can only do so in humility, recognizing that they shoulder the burden, from which we are exempt, of implementing solutions to problems which are ours as well as theirs. It is no use telling them that, in the world of which we—and they—dream, problems such as Congo would not arise. In today's world the problem has arisen and the statesman has to find today's solution, pending the arrival of a brighter tomorrow. We cannot even claim that we, or the Christian Church as a whole, did much to avert the Congo crisis, however nobly Catholic and Protestant missionaries may now be redeeming past mistakes by sharing with the Congolese people the sufferings of independence. We cannot even propose for the situation as it now exists the non-violent solution which is so dear to our hearts. If we put this forward as a "counsel of profit"—not a moral gesture, but a policy for today—we must admit that it would require a large body of dedicated, French-speaking saints whose rapid recruitment is beyond our resources and our capacity. To make this painful admission is to put ourselves in the position of the statesman struggling to find the next turning in the path through the political jungle; and we shall achieve our meeting of minds around Newman's prayer: "Lead, kindly Light, amid the encircling gloom . . . one step enough for me . . .".

It is at this point that we may be able to insist that the problems which we face together can only be solved by the exercise of forbearance and by the abandonment of the dogmatic approach which, in offering a ready-made answer to human problems, actually makes solution more remote. We have to recognize that we avoid becoming dogmatic ourselves only by constantly remembering the weakness and the ignorance which we share with all mankind and by turning again and again to the kindly light for guidance. If this is our approach we are justified in challenging the pretentious, self-satisfied dogmas of the day, whether Marxist or capitalist, racialist or anti-colonialist, with the words of Cromwell to the Scots before the battle of Dunbar: "I beseech you in the bowels of Christ, think it possible you may be mistaken." Cromwell spoke these words with the compassion to which he was not a total stranger, for he wished to spare his dogmatic opponents the ignominy of defeat. We must repeat his plea with compassion, for we ask statesmen to abandon those habits of thought in which they have sheltered from the stormy blast under the mistaken impression that they have found an "eternal home".

If we must exercise compassion in this matter, how much more so when we accompany statesmen on the path of negotiation which we have urged them to tread. There will be times when we can proceed through level fields of compromise towards the goal of agreement, only to find ourselves suddenly confronted by some Rubicon at which a choice has to be made between the successful outcome of the negotiations and the maintenance of a cherished principle. We can offer to statesmen a far better means than the dice which Caesar used to seek divine guidance, and we can ask that they turn to it for strength of spirit as they face the agony of choice; but the agony itself neither we nor they can escape. Consider the basis of the peace which we now enjoy in Korea, in Vietnam and in Germany, a peace purchased for us at the price of justice. If we are able to live in freedom and unity it is in part because other peoples have had to accept that their country, and in consequence their families, their loyalties and their loves, are divided by a barrier, imposed by others, which becomes more and more impenetrable with the passage of time. It may well be that in these instances peace was the paramount necessity and the price worth paying; but let us not for a moment suppose that the statesmen who agreed that this price should be paid could do so without an agony of spirit which will persist long after the choice has been made. So long as it has to be obtained at the expense of the happiness of a people—that is to say at the expense of justice—peace must be made in sorrow, not in triumph.

The agony of these situations has arisen from the application of the rough justice of compromise, the best that statesmanship could achieve. How much greater the agony which we all have to share as we consider situations where even that amount of justice still eludes the human grasp. How can full justice be done to the Arab and the Jew, to the Moslem and the French in Algeria, to the Chinese on the mainland and the Chinese in Formosa, to the Afrikaner and the Bantu? On what terms can we picture a just compromise between the Arab—who, deprived of his land and without the company of the village to which he belongs, wanders like a lost soul—and the Jew, driven by a barbarous Europe to seek the redemption of

Israel in a country he is fashioning himself? Unless we appreciate the intensity of passion with which these causes are defended we shall not be able to understand the predicament of the statesmen called upon to find a settlement, nor to gauge the immensity of the gulf which the reconciling spirit has eventually to bridge. It is easy to under-estimate this gulf; it is easier still to solve the problem by reserving our compassion for one of the two sides to the conflict. Of all the peoples engaged in these conflicts, the French in North Africa may seem to make the least call upon us; yet the call is there. A Friend who visited Tunisia recently talked with a Frenchman, born and bred in that country, who admitted that his future must lie elsewhere; and as he made this admission he looked about him and sighed: "Ah! How I love this country!" If, for the sake of peace, we must ask him to forsake his love, can we do so without compassion? Can we forget that the peace which ends these conflicts will not bring universal joy, but will offer to some nothing but the bitterness of exile? Can we bring comfort to the losers without espousing their lost cause?

Our consideration of international affairs has brought us into the presence of human tragedies, for which only the things of the spirit can offer consolation. They are the bricks of which the institutions of peace must be built, "oft with bleeding hands and tears". How can we conclude but with words which, in the imagination of Virgil, were also spoken in Tunisia: *Sunt lacrimae rerum et mentem mortalia tangunt*,[1] words which do not translate but whose tears and pathos unite us with all the sorrows of humanity. But tears

[1] *Aeneid I*: 462.

do not always blind. We may shed them to wash the windows of the spirit that with a clearer vision and a surer sympathy we may take up again our unfinished task of declaring the glad tidings.

APPENDIX I

Extracts from William Penn's
Essay Towards the Present and Future Peace of Europe
(Chapters VII and VIII)

VII. OF THE COMPOSITION OF THESE IMPERIAL STATES

The composition and proportion of this Sovereign Part, or Imperial State, does, at the first look, seem to carry with it no small difficulty what votes to allow for the inequality of the princes and states.

(Penn then proceeds to calculate the number of votes that should be allowed to each sovereignty.)

. . .

The whole makes ninety. A great presence when they represent the fourth, and now the best and wealthiest part of the known world; where religion and learning, civility and arts have their seat and empire. But it is not absolutely necessary there should be always so many persons to represent the larger sovereignties; for the votes may be given by one man of any sovereignty as well as by ten or twelve: though the fuller the assembly of states is, the more solemn, effectual, and free the debates will be, and the resolutions must needs come with greater authority. The place of their first session should be central, as much as is possible, afterwards as they agree.

VIII. OF THE REGULATIONS OF THE IMPERIAL
STATES IN SESSION

To avoid quarrel for precedency, the room may be round, and have divers doors to come in and go out at, to prevent exceptions. If the whole number be cast in tens, each choosing one, they may preside by turns, to whom all speeches should be addressed, and who should collect the sense of the debates, and state the question for a vote, which, in my opinion, should be by the ballot after the prudent and commendable method of the Venetians: which, in a great degree, prevents the ill effects of corruption; because if any of the delegates of that high and mighty Estates could be so vile, false, and dishonourable as to be influenced by money, they have the advantage of taking their money that will give it them and of voting undiscovered to the interest of their principles and their own inclinations; as they that do understand the balloting box do very well know.

. . .
. . .

It seems to me that nothing in this Imperial Parliament should pass but by three quarters of the whole, at least seven above the balance. I am sure it helps to prevent treachery, because if money could ever be a temptation in such a court, it would cost a great deal of money to weigh down the wrong scale. All complaints should be delivered in writing in the nature of memorials and journals kept by a proper person, in a trunk or chest, which should have as many differing locks as there are tens in the states. And if there were a clerk for each ten, and a pew or table for those clerks in the assembly; and at the end of every session one out of each ten were appointed to examine and compare the journals of those clerks, and then lock them up as I have before expressed, it would be clear and satisfactory. And each sovereignty if they please, as is but very fit, may have an exemplification, or copy of the said memorials, and the journals of proceedings upon them. The liberty and rules of speech, to be sure, they cannot fail in, who will be wisest and noblest of each sovereignty, for its own honour and safety. If any difference can arise between those that come from the same sovereignty that then one of the major number do give the balance of that sovereignty. I should think it extremely necessary that every sovereignty should be present under great penalties, and that none leave the session without leave, till all be finished; and that neutralities in debates should by no means be endured: for any such latitude will quickly open a way to unfair proceedings, and be followed by a train, both of seen and unseen inconveniences. I will say little of the language in which the session of the Sovereign Estates should be held, but to be sure it must be in Latin or French; the first would be very well for civilians, but the last most easy for men of quality.

Appendix II

LIST OF ABBREVIATIONS USED IN THE TEXT

ECOSOC The Economic and Social Council, a main organ of United Nations.

FAO The Food and Agriculture Organization of United Nations, a Specialized Agency, with headquarters at Rome.

GATT The General Agreement on Tariffs and Trade, an international commercial treaty administered by an office in Geneva.

IBRD The International Bank for Reconstruction and Development, a Specialized Agency (usually known as the "Bank") with headquarters at Washington, D.C.

ICAO The International Civil Aviation Organization, a Specialized Agency with headquarters at Montreal.

ILO The International Labour Organization, a Specialized Agency with headquarters at Geneva.

IMCO The International Maritime Consultative Organization, a Specialized Agency with headquarters at London.

ITU The International Telecommunications Union, a Specialized Agency with headquarters at Geneva.

ONUC "Organization des Nations Unies au Congo", the title given to the Congo operation undertaken in July 1960.

OPEX Title of the UN programme of technical assistance in public administration, through the Provision of Operational, Executive and Administrative Personnel.

BUILDING THE INSTITUTIONS OF PEACE

UNEF The United Nations Emergency Force, the international force despatched to the Middle East as a result of the crisis of November 1956.

UNESCO The United Nations Educational, Scientific and Cultural Organization, a Specialized Agency with headquarters at Paris.

UNICEF The United Nations Children's Fund. The initials which stand for "United Nations International Children's Emergency Fund", a relief fund established after the war, had become so well known by the time the official title of the fund was changed that they have been retained for publicity purposes.

UPU The Universal Postal Union, a Specialized Agency with headquarters at Berne.

WHO The World Health Organization, a Specialized Agency with headquarters at Geneva.

WMO The World Meteorological Organization, a Specialized Agency with headquarters at Geneva.

Reference is also made to an organization which is not part of the United Nations family:

NATO The North Atlantic Treaty Organization.

SWARTHMORE LECTURES
PREVIOUS TO 1940

QUAKERISM: A RELIGION OF LIFE.
By RUFUS M. JONES, M.A., D.Litt. (Out of print.)
SPIRITUAL GUIDANCE IN THE EXPERIENCE OF THE SOCIETY OF FRIENDS. By WILLIAM C. BRAITHWAITE, B.A., LL.B.
THE COMMUNION OF LIFE.
By DR. JOAN M. FRY. Second Edition.
HUMAN PROGRESS AND THE INWARD LIGHT.
By THOMAS HODGKIN, D.C.L. (Out of print.)
THE NATURE AND PURPOSE OF A CHRISTIAN SOCIETY.
By T. R. GLOVER, M.A. Fourth Impression.
SOCIAL SERVICE: ITS PLACE IN THE SOCIETY OF FRIENDS.
By JOSHUA ROWNTREE. (Out of print.)
THE HISTORIC AND THE INWARD CHRIST.
By EDWARD GRUBB, M.A. (Out of print.)
THE QUEST FOR TRUTH.
By SILVANUS P. THOMPSON, F.R.S. Third Edition.
THE MISSIONARY SPIRIT AND THE PRESENT OPPORTUNITY.
By HENRY T. HODGKIN, M.A., M.B.
THE DAY OF OUR VISITATION. By WILLIAM LITTLEBOY.
THE NEW SOCIAL OUTLOOK. By LUCY FRYER MORLAND, B.A.
SILENT WORSHIP: THE WAY OF WONDER.
By L. VIOLET (HODGKIN) HOLDSWORTH. Third Impression.
QUAKERISM AND THE FUTURE OF THE CHURCH.
By HERBERT G. WOOD, M.A.
THE NATURE AND AUTHORITY OF CONSCIENCE.
By RUFUS M. JONES, M.A., D.Litt. (Out of print.)
THE LONG PILGRIMAGE: HUMAN PROGRESS IN THE LIGHT OF THE CHRISTIAN HOPE. By T. EDMUND HARVEY, M.A.
RELIGION AND PUBLIC LIFE. By CARL HEATH.
PERSONAL RELIGION AND THE SERVICE OF HUMANITY.
By HELEN M. STURGE.
THE INNER LIGHT AND MODERN THOUGHT.
By GERALD K. HIBBERT, M.A., B.D. Second Impression.
THE QUAKER MINISTRY. By JOHN W. GRAHAM, M.A.
THE THINGS THAT ARE BEFORE US.
By A. NEAVE BRAYSHAW, B.A., LL.B.
CHRIST AND THE WORLD'S UNREST. By H. T. SILCOCK, M.A.
THE LIGHT OF CHRIST. By JOHN S. HOYLAND, M.A.
SCIENCE AND THE UNSEEN WORLD.
By ARTHUR STANLEY EDDINGTON, F.R.S. Sixth Impression.
DEMOCRACY AND RELIGION: A STUDY IN QUAKERISM.
By DR. G. SCHULZE-GAEVERNITZ. Second Impression.
CREATIVE WORSHIP. By HOWARD H. BRINTON, Ph.D. Second Impression.
EDUCATION AND THE SPIRIT OF MAN. By FRANCIS E. POLLARD, M.A.
UNEMPLOYMENT AND PLENTY.
By SHIPLEY N. BRAYSHAW, M.I.Mech.E. Third Impression.
CHRIST, YESTERDAY AND TO-DAY.
By GEORGE B. JEFFERY, F.R.S. Second Impression.
OUR RESPONSE TO GOD. By WILLIAM E. WILSON, B.D. Second Impression.
TOWARDS A NEW MANNER OF LIVING.
By DR. HOWARD E. COLLIER. Second Impression.
RELIGION AND CULTURE. By CAROLINE C. GRAVESON, B.A.
DEMOCRATIC LEADERSHIP. By A. BARRAT BROWN, M.A.
THE TRUSTWORTHINESS OF RELIGIOUS EXPERIENCE.
By D. ELTON TRUEBLOOD, Ph.D. Second Impression.

GEORGE ALLEN AND UNWIN LTD

For Product Safety Concerns and Information please contact our EU
representative GPSR@taylorandfrancis.com
Taylor & Francis Verlag GmbH, Kaufingerstraße 24, 80331 München, Germany

www.ingramcontent.com/pod-product-compliance
Lightning Source LLC
Chambersburg PA
CBHW052133300426
44116CB00010B/1888